THE ALPINE GARDEN

Other Books by C. F. Walker

Young Gentlemen
Riverside Reflections
Chalk Stream Flies

THE ALPINE GARDEN

C. F. Walker

W. H. & L. COLLINGRIDGE LTD LONDON
TRANSATLANTIC ARTS NEW YORK

First published in 1954
by W. H. & L. Collingridge Ltd
Tavistock Street London WC2
and in the United States of America
by Transatlantic Arts Incorporated
Forest Hills New York
Printed and bound in England
by Fletcher and Son Ltd Norwich
and the Leighton-Straker
Bookbinding Co Ltd London

CONTENTS

COLOUR PLATES

FOREWORD

THERE ARE NOW plenty of excellent works of reference dealing with rock gardens and alpine plants available to the gardening public, ranging from Reginald Farrer's vast and immortal compendium, *The English Rock Garden*, down to the catalogues issued by nurserymen who cater specially for the alpine enthusiast. The present book is in no sense an attempt to add to their number, which would be both unnecessary and presumptuous. It seems to me, however, that every gardener of experience may—and indeed should—have some contribution to make as the result of his own successes and failures; particularly the latter, which may serve as a warning to others. There are, moreover, various aspects and byways of the fascinating pastime of rock gardening which have received comparatively little attention from our gardening writers. Approximately half of my book consists of the random reflections on these matters which have occurred to me from time to time since I constructed my first primitive alpine garden some twenty years ago.

The remaining chapters are devoted to the plants themselves. These do not, of course, include more than a small fraction of the plants available, or even of those with which I am personally familiar. But as this book is intended primarily for the gardener with little or no previous experience of alpines, it is to be hoped that these chapters will serve as a useful guide-post, without which he might easily become lost in the maze of botanical names with which the catalogues and standard works of reference abound. No one, not even Farrer himself, could grow in the span of his mortal life every alpine plant in cultivation, so that in any list which claims to be reasonably complete many of the descriptions must be compiled from other sources. In the present book I make no such attempt, but confine my attention to the species which I have grown myself, selecting from the mass of good, bad and indifferent plants which have come my way those which have afforded me the greatest pleasure.

Some years ago, when I owned a small commercial nursery, I made the discovery that many people were deterred from growing alpines by a fear of their unfamiliar botanical names. Why, I was sometimes asked, must the alpine enthusiast wallow in polysyllabic tongue-twisters—and in a dead language, at that—instead of referring to his plants in plain English which everyone could understand? The answer is that the rock gardener, unlike most of his colleagues in other branches of horticulture, is dealing chiefly with species; that is to say, plants of pure blood which are found growing wild in some part of the world. As the great majority of them are not natives of England, there are no English names for them. Why should there be? It would be as reasonable to expect, say, the Peruvians to have a vernacular name for a common English wildflower which does not grow in Peru.

As a matter of fact every gardener, even the veriest tyro, is constantly using botanical names, possibly without realizing the fact. Anemone, aster, campanula, crocus, delphinium, narcissus, phlox, primula, salvia, viola and a whole host of other familiar names have now become virtually a part of the English language, yet they are nevertheless undiluted Latin or Greek. These, however, are all generic names, denoting whole groups of plants with similar characteristics. To distinguish one plant from another, a second name becomes necessary, and this, I believe, is what proves the stumbling block for many people. For whereas annuals, border perennials and roses, which are mostly hybrids, are given 'fancy' names such as Excelsior, Pink Perfection or Mrs. So-and-So, the distinguishing names of species are derived from Latin or Greek. These are based either on the country of origin, the name of the discoverer, or some special peculiarity of the plant which separates it from its fellows (e.g. *Gentiana acaulis*: the stemless gentian.) Such names, moreover, have the advantage of being internationally recognized, whereas vernacular names must necessarily be confined to their own country, and even so they may vary in different districts, as happens with our own harebell and bluebell.

The snobbish prejudice against hybrids which marked the alpine gardener of Edwardian days, is, however, fast receding before the tide of new and ever more beautiful garden forms raised in our nurseries. To distinguish the different varieties of these plants it is usual—indeed obligatory—to use English names preceded by the x sign to denote a cross. These, of course, present no difficulty, but I venture to predict that in quite a short time even the beginner will find himself reeling off the Latin names with no more trouble than the English ones. Familiarity is the best cure for this kind of phobia, and the process will be hastened if the gardener acquaints himself with the meaning and derivation of the names. There are several reference books devoted to this subject, of which I have found *Plant Names Simplified*, by A. T. Johnson and H. A. Smith, both interesting and helpful.

My more advanced readers for whom botanical names hold no terrors will, I hope, forgive this somewhat lengthy dissertation on what must seem to them an elementary and self-evident subject. I have, however, felt it desirable to clear up what is evidently a widespread misconception, and to absolve myself in advance of possible accusations of pedantry— or even of 'showing off'—on account of the Greek and Latin names with which my pages are unavoidably besprinkled. I have deliberately avoided the use of those rather self-conscious English names for foreign plants coined by what Farrer contemptuously termed the 'Wardour Street Ruskinian school.' But with the few native plants which are grown in our rock gardens, such as the Spring Gentian and the Cheddar Pink, I have included the English names as evidence of my good intentions.

For most of the chapters which follow I have drawn freely on articles of mine which have appeared in *The Field*, *Gardening Illustrated* and *The Bulletin of the Alpine Garden Society*. I take this opportunity of expressing my thanks to the Editors of these periodicals for their kind permission to make use of this material.

The illustrations at the ends of the chapters and on the title page are from *Les Plantes Alpines* by B. Verlot (Paris, 1873), *The Annals of Horticulture* (London, 1846), *Alpine Flowers for Gardens* by William Robinson (London, 1870) and *The Gardener's Assistant* by Robert Thomson (London, 1881).

Tillington, Sussex   C. F. WALKER
December 1953

CHAPTER ONE

PRELIMINARY PLANS

MOST GARDEN OWNERS expend considerable time and thought on the planning of their flower beds and borders, even to the extent of making (or, if they are lazy, acquiring from their nurserymen) elaborate paper plans on which the exact position of each group of plants is marked out beforehand. Yet how many, I wonder, devote even a small amount of forethought to the planting of a rock garden? To judge by results, I should say that most people wait until the plants actually arrive and then just pop them in wherever they seem to fit.

Admittedly, the rock garden planner is faced with a more difficult task than his fellow on the flat; for not only is he working in three dimensions instead of two, but his plans are also complicated by the presence of an additional element in the shape of rock. Furthermore, he must take into account the individual likes and dislikes of his plants, which in the bed or border are assumed to be approximately identical. For these very reasons, however, it becomes more than ever necessary to prepare a planting scheme in advance if the best results, both from the horticultural and aesthetic angles, are to be achieved.

I am not concerned for the moment with the choice and placing of the rocks themselves—a formidable subject which I will touch upon in a later chapter—but am assuming that these are already in position. Before deciding where the plants are to go, it is important to appreciate that the large group of dwarf perennials loosely described as 'alpine and rock plants' includes many species and hybrids differing widely in character, requirements and natural habitat. Some of them come to us from the high mountain crags, others from the screes, the stony foothills, the alpine and subalpine pastures, and even from the forests and sea-shores. Their geographical distribution, moreover, covers every continent and nearly every country of the globe; yet we expect them all to make themselves equally at home in the same few square yards of English garden! To me, the amazing thing is that so many of them do so, but although we cannot, of course, hope to simulate the conditions to which they are accustomed, we can at least show them the courtesy due to visitors from foreign lands by studying, within the limits of our resources, their natural preferences.

Short of building a relief model, it is impossible to make an adequate plan of the rock garden with all its varying contours, gradients and aspects. For this reason it is probably better to prepare the alpine planting scheme in tabular form, rather than to attempt a scale plan on the lines of those employed for the herbaceous border. Many years ago, when I first became seriously interested in alpines, I drew up a most elaborate table in which all the plants I proposed to grow were shown under various cross-headings such as their country of origin, character, habitat and colour, together with the most suitable soil and situation for each. Nearly every plant thus fell automatically into its appointed place, and I acquired much useful (and no doubt a good deal of useless) information in the process. Looking back from the standpoint of maturer years, I think this was making too much of a business of my hobby; yet although I can now laugh at it as a youthful folly, I still believe that the underlying idea was the right one and that a modified version of such a table can be extremely useful.

In planning the rock garden, a good working knowledge of alpine plants—even if, to start with, it is only book knowledge—is almost essential. Their cultural requirements will, of course, be the first consideration, but the aesthetic aspect should by no means be ignored. For instance, since our highest peak is no more than a few feet above ground level, it can make little or no difference to the plants themselves whether we set them at the top or lower down, assuming that the whole site is properly drained. Yet by paying some attention to their relative positions and avoiding such incongruities as the sight of a high alpine androsace nestling uneasily between a plant from the Mediterranean shores and another from far eastern forests, we can at all events preserve some illusion of the natural scene. After all, rock gardening is no more than a glorified version of a child's game of make-believe!

In the rock gardens seen at flower shows, a large number of plants of a single species are generally massed together, for the good reason that this is the most effective way for the nurseryman to display his wares. Just as Hitler held that a thumping big lie, if repeated often enough, would eventually gain credence, so the plant salesman appreciates that a good big clump in which the same plant is repeated over and over again makes the most forcible impact on the mind of the gardening public. In this he is perfectly right, but it does not follow that this is the best way of planting our own gardens.

A bold group of one species set here and there in the little bays and plateaux between rocks certainly looks very effective, but if this method of planting is adhered to throughout, the result looks uncomfortably like a bedding-out scheme in three dimensions. In the wild state many of these clumps would have spilled over, as seedlings, on to lower levels (as in the course of time some of them will do in our gardens), and a few irregularities of this kind may be deliberately introduced with pleasing effect. In the valleys and open spaces, however, I prefer a still more informal scheme on the lines of Farrer's 'interwoven carpet'. A small nucleus of each species, with outlying specimens spreading into and intermingling with the adjacent groups, as they do in the alpine meadows, produces a much more natural and attractive effect than a series of groups carefully segregated from one another. But Nature employs both bold splashes of colour and tapestry effects to delight our eyes, and subject to the artificial limitations of the garden, we cannot do better than take her as our model.

The number of plants of each species to be used depends on individual preference and the total area available for planting. Personally, I like to have at least three of a kind, if only to allow for casualties, and many more than this of my special favourites. Their eventual spread must, however, be taken into account, remembering that where, for example, a single clump of *Dianthus caesius* would make a satisfactory showing, it would take three or four plants of *D. arvernensis* and perhaps a dozen of *D. Freynii* to fill the same place. Care in planning is also necessary to ensure that the dwarfer treasures do not ultimately become swamped by more rampageous neighbours, for nothing is more galling than to discover the corpse of some unfortunate member of the *haute noblesse* beneath the trampling feet of the *canaille*. Here again, a knowledge of the plants we wish to grow is invaluable.

A detailed consideration of suitable soil for individual alpines is outside the scope of this book, but their requirements, which are to be found in the many excellent works of reference now available, should of course be taken into account in the planning stage. Broadly speaking, they may be divided into lime-lovers (mostly Europeans) and lime-haters (mostly Asiatics), and although the majority will be perfectly happy in a neutral soil, the extremists of both parties must be catered for. As the calciophiles are in the majority, I generally dig plenty of crushed mortar rubble into the main part of the rock garden and set aside a separate slope filled with a sand and peat mixture for such things as the Asiatic gentians, primulas and ericaceous shrubs.

I end this chapter on a note of caution. The newly planted rock garden makes considerable demands on the faith, hope and imagination of its owner. If due allowance has been made for the ultimate spread of the plants, it looks so desperately barren; so unlike that riot of colour we are accustomed to see on the bank at Chelsea, where the plants jostle each other cheek by jowl (and a tell-tale glimpse of red sometimes shows that they are still in their pots). It seems impossible to believe that these little wisps of greenery, no larger than ping-pong balls, received from the nurserymen may some day grow as big as soup plates. Yet if the garden has been carefully planned and planted it is surprising how soon it achieves a furnished appearance. After a year it no longer resembles the face of a schoolboy recently treated for scrum-pox, and by the end of the second season the quicker-growing plants will have joined hands across the barren wastes. Thereafter—though there will inevitably be casualties which must be replaced from time to time—it will soon assume the established mien of an old county family, and then it is that the care and forethought of the planner will reap their due reward.

CHAPTER TWO

STRAW WITHOUT BRICKS

ONE OF THE chief drawbacks to making a rock garden is the comparatively heavy cost of the initial preparations. So many ingredients are required, the majority of which are unnecessary in the herbaceous border, shrub garden and annual beds. Consider the materials generally deemed essential for the cultivation of alpines: sand, peat, leaf-mould, mortar rubble, stone chippings, drainage rubble and rock. Even in quite a small garden these items run the owner into considerable expense before ever a plant is ordered from the nurseryman.

As a matter of melancholy interest, I have just been looking up the cost of these things in the old days and comparing them with the prices obtaining today. Going back first of all to the period before the Kaiser's war, I consulted Meredith's book, *Rock Gardens*, which was first published in 1910 and devotes a whole chapter to the subject of expense. It makes nostalgic reading in 1953. Sand, I found, cost four shillings per load; peat, five-and-sixpence for twelve hundredweight; rock and broken stones, three-and-sixpence a ton. Admittedly this was in Ireland, where labour may have been cheaper than in England, but even so . . .

I next turned to the period between the wars, by which time prices had, of course, risen, though to nothing like the alarming extent we have witnessed since the Hitler trouble. In some old nursery catalogues of the late 'thirties the following prices are quoted: sand, half-a-crown to three shillings; peat, three shillings; chippings, half-a-crown; all per bushel. Weathered limestone; first quality seventeen shillings, second quality fifteen shillings per ton. Even at that date, it seems, one could lay out quite a fair-sized rock garden without being in the surtax class.

In 1950, when I last had occasion to buy these things, a load of washed sand (the equivalent of four cubic yards) cost me two pounds, nine shillings; peat and leaf-mould, from twelve to eighteen shillings a hundredweight; limestone chippings, from ten to fifteen shillings a bushel; local sandstone, four pounds per ton—and no doubt all these prices have risen still higher since then. As for weathered limestone, as there is none to be had within several hundred miles of my garden in Sussex, I have neither troubled nor dared to enquire the cost of importing it.

During the corresponding period the cost of the plants themselves has risen only a mere hundred per cent; so as plants we must obviously have, it seems worth while to consider whether we can forgo any of the more expensive materials without detriment to the garden. In one respect the modern alpine gardener has an advantage over his forbears: he places far less importance on the need for special soil mixtures to suit each individual plant. Indeed, few people in these strenuous days have the time to waste in fussing with the 'prepared pockets' so beloved of Edwardian enthusiasts, so we should be able to save something here.

My own practice in the matter of soil ingredients is simple, and reminds me of a true story of my father's concerning an old naval surgeon of the mid-nineteenth century. He kept only four bottles of medicine in his sick bay, labelled respectively FORETOP, MAINTOP, FO'C'S'LE and QUARTERDECK. When a sailor reported sick, he was merely asked to which part of the ship he belonged, given a dose from the corresponding bottle, and sent on his way perfectly satisfied. In like manner, newcomers to my garden are asked, 'lime, no lime, sun or shade?' and are then shoved into the appropriate section, where more often than not they prove entirely happy.

Notwithstanding this welcome tendency towards simplification, however, there are still several items which must be regarded as essential to the average rock garden. Sand we can hardly do without on all but the lightest soils; peat and leaf-mould may be regarded as interchangeable, but one or other—the former for choice—we must have. Drainage material cannot be dispensed with except on a steep bank above the level of the rest of the garden, while stone chippings and mortar rubble are highly desirable, if not actually essential. This leaves only rock; generally the most expensive item of all.

Now a ton of rock sounds quite a lot, but in practice it does not go very far: say, ten large stones or twenty medium size or forty small ones. At the rate at which most people use rock, five tons would be a by no means excessive allowance for a garden of quite moderate dimensions. At today's price this means an outlay of some twenty pounds; the equivalent of 266 alpine plants at one-and-sixpence apiece. Is it worth it?

I sometimes wonder whether the owners of rock gardens ever pause to consider why they use rocks at all. Some, perhaps, do so in the belief that rocks have some aesthetic value in themselves—which is rarely so with quarried stone—but I suspect that the great majority are merely following convention, possibly with a vague idea that rocks are in some way necessary for the welfare of the plants. So far as some of the high

Left :
Anemone vernalis

Right :
Saxifraga Aizoon

alpines are concerned this may be true, for in their native haunts they are accustomed to the cool root-run provided by the crevices between the mountain crags. These, however, are chiefly the prerogative of the specialist, and by far the greater number of plants grown in the average rock garden come to us from the alpine and subalpine pastures—the equivalent of our own meadows and downland turf—where they flourish happily without any rock at all. Yet as soon as they arrive in Surrey or Sussex they are thrust between hard slabs of stone, in the pathetic belief that it will make them feel at home. Could anything be more foolish?

The man who invented the term 'rock garden' should have been buried up to his neck in stone and left to die, but even this fate is too comfortable for the perpetrator of 'rockery'. Between them—unless they were one and the same person—they were responsible for one of the most hideous and unnatural features of the English garden of today. For, having become accustomed to such terms as rose garden, fruit garden, shrubbery and fernery as denoting places set apart for the cultivation of these plants, the general gardening public seems to have assumed—not without some justification—that a rock garden or rockery is a site consecrated to the display of rocks. True, even the rockiest of rockeries generally shows some faint traces of vegetation, though seemingly often only added as an afterthought and a sop to convention. Frame and picture have become transposed.

This will be the last time I shall inflict the term 'rockery' on my readers, and when I first planned this book I determined that 'rock garden' should likewise be banished from its pages. On maturer consideration, however, I came to the conclusion that the alternative of 'alpine garden', which I greatly prefer, might savour of the pedantic, besides possibly frightening some beginners who had grown accustomed to the more usual term and in its absence might wrongly assume that I was writing only for alpine specialists. Having registered my protest, therefore, I shall, after all, abide by convention, while reserving to myself the right to employ 'alpine garden' as an occasional alternative.

As the upshot of this seeming digression, I venture to suggest that we might well dispense with rocks altogether without incurring the displeasure of the plants and, in the majority of cases, with benefit to the appearance of our gardens. This would also save more than half the initial outlay, leaving more money to be spent on plants.

Most of those alpines which need the association of rock for the good of their health will be quite happy if we bury a few sharp stones about them and surface the soil with limestone or granite chippings according to their needs. For the remainder, I suggest that the 'alpine meadow' is the effect to be aimed at. This should not be confused with the 'alpine lawn'; a term employed by nurserymen for the purpose of selling the so-called carpeting plants such as thyme, frankenia and the mat-forming veronicas. I am not thinking of these, but of the ordinary run of alpines and subalpines, together with the host of dwarf perennials loosely described as rock plants, of a kind fit to associate with them. In this way a delightful effect can be obtained, and the plants both look and thrive better than if they are jammed in between masses of rock which are quite alien to them.

I am, of course, aware that the notion of growing alpines without rocks has been tentatively put forward in more than one book, but only as a *dernier ressort*. The authors make it plain that they do not think much of the idea, and make haste to cover their tracks with plenty of photographs and diagrams of rock gardens simply plastered with rocks. Old customs die hard, and until some enterprising landscape gardener lays out a rockless 'rock garden' on the bank at Chelsea and thus brings home its possibilities to the gardening public, we shall continue to see the sorry spectacle of rows of little gardens disfigured by petrified hummocks.

The shackles of convention are strong, and I admit that it takes some courage to plump for 100% plants and 0% rocks. Here, then, is a slight modification of the idea which occurred to me a short time ago. Just outside my front gate is a large sandstone boulder, some fifteen feet in height, which was presumably exposed when the road was made and now forms an integral part of a retaining wall supporting a path leading up to the church. I must have passed it hundreds of times before it suddenly occurred to me that it would make a magnificent foundation for an alpine garden on a grand scale. Needless to say, like the only rising trout whenever I go fishing, it was just on the wrong side of the boundary, and a hasty search of an overgrown bank on my own side failed to reveal any similar geological feature. Nevertheless, it had given me an idea.

Instead of using several scores of stones of the usual size, why not, I said to myself, have just one monster—a real great-grandfather of a rock —and use this as the central feature of the alpine garden? It is generally possible to choose one's stone at the quarry, so it would be a simple matter to pick the biggest and best-looking boulder available and order it to be delivered as near as possible to the site. I am not, of course, visualizing anything approaching the size of the giant outside my gate, but just a hefty chunk of rock a good deal bigger than those normally sold for rock garden work.

Here let me say that the problem of handling a big stone is not nearly so formidable as might be supposed, provided that the gardener is blessed with a little ingenuity. A lot can be done by means of wooden rollers, and if the rock has to be lifted it is quite an easy matter to rig a small 'sheerlegs', consisting of three stout poles securely lashed together at the top in the form of a tripod. The local builder could doubtless be prevailed upon to lend the lifting tackle, which is hooked on to a strop at the apex of the pyramid. By this means the very largest rock you are likely to be able to buy can be placed in the desired position without the risk of rupture, so long as you do not try to hurry things. But if this should prove beyond your powers, I can only recommend you to order a firkin of ale to be dumped beside the rock, and then go out into the highways and byways and rope in the toughest-looking helpers you can find.

The position for the big boulder should be chosen with care. It should not, of course, rear itself heavenwards from a flat piece of ground like one of those 'follies' of our Victorian forbears, but should, if possible, be partially buried in the side of a sloping bank so as to look like a natural outcrop. The top could be planted with dwarf cushion-forming species of the kind found on the high summits in nature, while around and below it would come the alpine meadows, devoid of all stone. It would then be a simple matter to extend the garden in any direction at a later date without spoiling the whole effect, as is liable to happen when additions are made to the ordinary rock garden.

The cost of a single large rock would surely be a good deal less than that of several tons of smaller ones, and the effect would be both bold and original. The actual size and shape of the boulder would depend, of course, on the area and configuration of the site. If the rock garden was quite a small one, a stone of quite moderate dimensions would suffice; in a larger garden, two rocks of medium size might be used, with a wide valley in between; on a flat site, a large flattish slab would look better than a tall rock. These and many other variations of the theme will suggest themselves to the ingenious gardener according to the nature of the ground at his disposal.

The chief thing to bear in mind is to resist all temptation to include any smaller stones in a scheme of this kind. If any such are lying about it would be better to cast them into the nearest pond rather than to risk spoiling the whole effect by strewing them round the foot of the centre piece. The alpine hayfield should contain hay and hay only.

CHAPTER THREE

CAUTIONARY TALES

ALTHOUGH I AM a whole-hearted enthusiast for the works of Reginald Farrer (and who could fail to fall under his magic spell?), I always feel that his advice on the construction of the rock garden has led many of his followers into error. I may be wrong, but it appears to me that his pronouncements on the subject were based chiefly on his experience at Ingleborough, in the west of Yorkshire, whereas subsequent writers have assumed them to be of general application.

Take, for example, Farrer's remarks in *The English Rock Garden* on the best kind of stone to employ. After reviewing the merits and demerits of the different varieties, he concludes: 'For the triumphant achievement of such a scheme, however, the rock gardener will always and only seek for limestone.'

This, of course, is an admirable piece of advice for those who live in the north and west where limestone is abundant and therefore not only relatively easy and cheap to obtain, but what is perhaps still more important, entirely in keeping with the surroundings. Unfortunately, however, a large number of English rock gardeners are compelled by force of circumstances to conduct their operations in counties where limestone is non-existent. For this body of enthusiasts, limestone (even if they can afford to import it from afar) can never by any possible stretch of the imagination furnish the 'dignified and immemorial-looking scheme' envisaged by Farrer. Yet one not infrequently sees limestone formations dumped down on the sands of Surrey or the clays of Sussex; quite artistic creations in themselves, maybe, yet jarring to the eye of the beholder. For although there may be no visible rock in the surrounding countryside, the trees and other vegetation, if nothing else, proclaim that no limestone could conceivably exist in the neighbourhood unless placed there by the hand of man.

For this state of affairs it must be confessed that those artists who design the wonderful limestone gardens at Chelsea are partly to blame. Many a visitor, standing entranced before one of these works of art, no doubt comes away with the resolve to reproduce it, anyhow on a miniature scale, in his garden in one of the Home Counties, though he would probably never dream of buying a wholly unsuitable picture for his study wall. It is as well, then, to view Chelsea in the same spirit as one views the Royal Academy, and to remember that one is looking at pictures divorced, as it were, from their proper contexts.

To return to Farrer—and I hope I shall not be accused of *lèse-majesté*—what misplaced enthusiasm, to say nothing of expense, might have been saved by the substitution of the word 'local' for 'lime' (stone) in the sentence I have quoted! True, this would have presented certain difficulties for some. Chalk, for instance, can only be used if, like Colonel Stern at Highdown in Sussex, one happens to have a natural chalk cliff in one's garden, while granite is difficult to build satisfactorily and unprofitable, if not positively inimical, to plant life. Alpine gardeners who live in districts where either of these abound might, therefore, do well to follow the advice in the preceding chapter and dispense with rock altogether. Fortunately, however, large slabs of England are composed of sandstone in one or other of its various forms, some of which are easily obtained, pleasing to the plants, and quite attractive to the eye: certainly more attractive than limestone in the wrong place.

The chief trouble about sandstone, and one which may have deterred many people from using it, is that no one seems to have made a study of its correct method of employment; or, if so, he has kept the information to himself. True, an occasional garden architect, more enterprising than the rest, has laid out a sandstone formation on the bank at Chelsea, and Captain Symons-Jeune has devoted a brief chapter to the subject in his interesting book, *Natural Rock Gardening*. Even so, the seeker after truth is left little the wiser, beyond the facts that (*a*) sandstone never outcrops and (*b*) it is generally found with heather and pines growing on the top.

I would go further, and say that sandstone is seldom seen at all except where it has been exposed by the hand of man in the form of quarries, road and railways cuttings and the like. To alpine enthusiasts in sandstone districts, therefore, I commend the idea of building the rock garden in the form of a cutting, with miniature cliffs on either side. As it would be difficult to maintain a sufficient depth of soil all over the upper surface of the rock, I suggest topping off with some old, rotted turves, sifting a little soil over these, and planting with various forms of *Thymus serpyllum*, which makes an admirable 'scale model' heather in keeping with the size of the cliffs likely to be seen in the average rock garden. *Erinus alpinus* and its varieties also look remarkably like heather from a little distance and I have used them for this purpose myself, but of course they do not form a quickly spreading mat like the thymes, and they are little more than biennials. Further back one could plant a few dwarf conifers of suitable size and habit to represent the pine-woods generally found in such situations, while the alpine plants themselves would go on the ledges, in the crevices, and at the foot of the cliffs. It should be possible to create a most attractive scene in this way, and one, moreover, in keeping with its surroundings.

Consider next the moraine, or scree, as it is now more often termed. Although it was not actually invented by Farrer, his description of the 'baby moraine' in the New Garden at Ingleborough must certainly have done much to popularize this feature of the alpine garden. At all events, nearly every subsequent writer has hailed the moraine as the final solution of all the alpine gardener's problems. If a plant fails to thrive in ordinary soil, they proclaim, you have but to put it in the scree and the only further trouble it will give you is in hacking chunks of it away to prevent it from encroaching on its neighbours.

There was a time when I was sufficiently naive to believe in the moraine as a magic cure-all for every ill, and even until a few years ago I accepted without question the theory that certain plants would thrive better under scree conditions than in the usual rock garden soil. An experiment conducted shortly after the war, however, finally shattered this illusion.

After demolishing an old lean-to greenhouse in my garden, I found myself left with three low stone walls thus ⌊__⌋, which only needed the addition of a fourth wall to give me a kind of giant trough, measuring some 20 ft. by 4 ft. and 2 ft. in depth. As I had recently moved into my present home, I decided that this would make admirable temporary quarters for my collection of alpines, pending the construction of a new rock garden. I therefore divided the trough transversely into four compartments: two large ones for lime-lovers and lime-haters respectively, and two smaller ones for their moraine counterparts. As it happened, I was unable to obtain any granite chippings at the time, so that one of the smaller compartments was left empty. The other was filled with the usual scree mixture consisting of five parts of limestone chippings to one part of sand and leaf-mould, overlying an adequate depth of sharp stones to provide the drainage. Into this went the various campanulas, dianthus, drabas, androsaces and other small fry generally reputed to enjoy semi-starvation, while the rest of the lime-lovers occupied the adjacent saloon where a more satisfying menu was provided.

The result, I must confess, surprised me. Although arrangements had been made to water the moraine from below through short lengths of drainpipe driven into the soil, it soon became evident that its inhabitants were far from happy. Their neighbours in the grill-room, on the other hand, immediately waxed fat and prosperous, and where I had put plants of the same species into each compartment for the sake of comparison, those in the ordinary rock garden soil did far better in every way. Eventually the contrast became so marked that I fell upon the moraine in exasperation, dug up its residents, and flung half the chippings into the spare compartment next door, filling up the space left thereby with a mixture of loam, leaf-mould and sand. These new ingredients were then well mixed with the remaining chippings, which now formed only fifty per cent of the whole, and the plants put back to bed. Almost immediately, it seemed, they responded to the change of diet, and within a few weeks they were obviously feeling much more at home.

Now this experiment was carried out in a hot Sussex garden facing due south—a far cry from the cool, clammy conditions of West Yorkshire. It seems, therefore, not unreasonable to conclude that Farrer's prescription for the scree, while eminently suited to Ingleborough, is altogether too spartan for the drier counties of the south and east of England. At all events, my screes, if such they can still be termed, have since then contained no more than half their volume of stone chips at the very outside, and I sometimes wonder whether even this proportion is not too high for this warm corner of the country. In fairness to Farrer, it must be admitted that after recommending the $\frac{5}{6}/\frac{1}{6}$ mixture, he goes on to say: '$\frac{1}{4}$ of soil to $\frac{3}{4}$ of chips makes a richer compound, and $\frac{1}{2}$ soil, $\frac{1}{2}$ chips results in a yet more comfortable and certain success everywhere.' But if it was his intention that the mixture should be varied according to climate, he did not make this sufficiently clear to keep his successors from falling into the error of repeating the first part of his recommendation and entirely ignoring the qualifying remarks.

Lastly, I am going to be rash enough to issue a warning on the matter of drainage which is at variance with everything I have ever read on the subject. 'This,' wrote Farrer, referring to drainage, 'is the alpha and omega of success.' 'Drainage, drainage, drainage,' has echoed every subsequent writer on rock gardening, implying, if not actually stating, that it cannot possibly be overdone. Well, it can: I have done it myself.

The disaster—for to me it was nothing less—occurred just before the war when I built a rock garden in Surrey, on a steepish bank sloping down to a pond. The site appeared so ideal that I accepted the fact that the soil was rather on the stiff side and went ahead, skimping no detail of the preparatory work in order, as I fondly imagined, to ensure success. In addition to lightening the soil itself by digging in all the leaf-mould, sand and stone chippings I could lay hands upon, I made certain that nothing should be found wanting in the way of perfect drainage, and that every drop of surplus moisture should find its way by the shortest possible route into the pond.

When the work was at length completed, I felt more than satisfied; even, I fear, smugly complacent at the thought that I had made such a thorough job of it. The final step was to plant my alpines, sinking pipes round those species which enjoy damp feet (and with the pond but a few yards away there was never any excuse for not keeping these topped up). I then sat back to await results, which I confidently expected to surpass anything I had previously achieved. Before the end of the summer all except the most hard-baked sunbathers had incontinently perished—from drought. And the reason, I have no possible doubt, was that, so far as that particular site was concerned, I had overdone the drainage. Like the Light Brigade, I had paused not to reason why, but obeyed orders to the letter, thereby plunging headlong to disaster.

The moral of all this, of course, is that written instructions on building the rock garden and preparing the site should be interpreted with intelligence and adapted to one's own special circumstances. Probably no single writer has had first-hand experience of making rock gardens in the north, south, east and west, and when you consider the difference in soil and climate between, say, Cumberland and Surrey or Cornwall and Suffolk, the absurdity of attempting to lay down universal rules for the whole of the British Isles at once becomes apparent. This, I feel certain, was never Farrer's intention, and indeed when dealing with the cultivation of particular species he frequently made allowance for varying conditions in different parts of the country. But so far as constructional work is concerned, he seems to have been thinking in terms of Ingleborough, and in following his instructions too literally, the succeeding generation of gardening writers has been led astray.

CHAPTER FOUR

THE VALUE OF CHIPPINGS

From the point of view of an alpine plant, a cross section of the rock garden below ground resembles that of a sandwich, in which the lower slice of bread represents the drainage rubble; the jam, the soil about its roots; and the top slice, that narrow horizontal layer which surrounds its neck. Much has been written about the two lower layers, but the top one, which is of at least equal importance, has been somewhat neglected.

Although it is true that alpines have a strong dislike of stagnant moisture at their roots, it should not be forgotten that it is the junction of roots with crown that constitutes the chief danger point. However sharp and plentiful the drainage, the topmost layer of soil, in a wet winter, must be permanently clammy, and it is my belief that this is the cause of many alpine casualties. Fortunately, however, there is a simple remedy for this, which consists of substituting stone chippings for soil as the top slice of the sandwich.

Every sink and alpine pan has its top dressing of chips, but these are far less often seen in the rock garden proper, except on the moraine, which is itself largely composed of chippings anyway. Possibly this is because most alpine nurserymen top-dress their exhibits at the flower shows with peat, which certainly looks well under cover in Vincent Square, but would be of no value for the purpose under discussion.

For a good many years now I have surfaced my rock garden with stone chippings, and I feel sure the winter mortality among my plants has been lighter than it was before I adopted this precaution. The procedure is quite simple. When planting a newly constructed rock garden I leave all the plants with their necks protruding an inch or so above the surrounding soil, and then strew the whole surface with chippings to this depth, tucking these well under their chins. A good soaking through a coarse rose then completes the job. In replacing casualties or adding plants to an established garden, it is only necessary to scrape back a small circle of chips, insert the plant, and finally replace the stones. I am certain the slight extra trouble involved is well worth while, and the additional cost is offset in the long run by the lighter casualty lists.

There are, furthermore, several other advantages to be derived from stone chippings as a top-dressing besides the one I have mentioned. In the first place, their property of conserving moisture is of considerable value during a dry spell, and reduces the need for the watering can. I once thought this was greatly exaggerated until, on putting a shovel into a heap of washed gravel which had been lying in my yard for several weeks during a hot summer, I found all but the outer layer of the heap as damp as on the day it arrived. On the face of things, this would seem to conflict with the advantage previously mentioned, but in practice damp stones do not have the same lethal effect on the plants as damp soil. In fact, the chippings share with a well-known brand of underwear the useful property of performing apparently opposite functions in winter and summer.

Secondly, for those who like to maintain a reserve stock of plants, there can be no doubt that self-sown seedlings are far more numerous than where the surface of the garden consists of ordinary soil. This is only to be expected when one remembers the enormous initial advantage possessed by a seed washed down beneath a comfortable coverlet of protecting chips, where it is safe from the ravages of wind, drought, birds and other foes, over its opposite number forced to take its chance in the open. The increased birth-rate in my own garden has been most marked since I began using surface chippings, and every autumn I am able to pot up a healthy batch of the natural progeny of many of my alpines without the necessity of fussing with seed pans or the labour of pricking out.

In theory, at all events, a surface of small, sharp stones should prevent the depredations of slugs—the chief enemy, in the animal kingdom, of alpine plants. This, I think, is true to a limited extent, but I have yet to discover the barrier which will stop a really determined slug from reaching a rare and expensive plant on which it has set its heart—if, indeed, such a low and revolting form of life can be said to possess this organ of affection. The more timid slugs, however, are probably discouraged by the chip-strewn surface and are more likely to satisfy their appetites elsewhere.

From the aesthetic standpoint, there can, I think, be no two opinions on the value of stone chippings. They do add very greatly to the appearance of the rock garden, and are particularly helpful in tiding it over that awkward period of adolescence before its inhabitants have overcome their shyness sufficiently to join hands in the floral dance. If used with intelligence, moreover, they can be made to convey the impression of large rock masses without the employment of many tons of expensive stone. Finally, they entirely eliminate that unsightly soil splash which, though it does not actually damage the plants, certainly mars one's enjoyment of those dwarf early-flowering subjects such as the soldanellas and Kabschia saxifrages.

On the debit side, stone chippings have one or two drawbacks, though none of them are very serious. Firstly, while they undoubtedly encourage seed germination, they do not, of course, discriminate between the seeds of weeds and those of precious alpines. More time, therefore, will need to be spent in keeping the chip-strewn garden clear of unwelcome plant intruders than where the surface consists of ordinary soil. If all weeds are destroyed before they reach the flowering stage, however, this drawback can be largely overcome.

Secondly, the pleasant habit possessed by certain plants of layering themselves is discouraged, since they require a finer rooting medium than the stones afford. If, however, it is desired to increase these stoloniferous plants, it is a simple matter to scrape shallow channels round their necks, laying the procumbent stems in a compost of sand and peat, after which the chippings are replaced, when they assist the rooting process by keeping the layers firm and moist.

One factor which has probably deterred many gardeners from using stone chippings in this manner is the difficulty of procuring them. I have heard of enthusiasts raiding those heaps which the County Councils leave so temptingly by the roadside; but apart from the more than doubtful morality of this procedure, such heaps are as likely as not to consist of flints, which the experts are unanimous in condemning as useless for our purpose. The seashore should likewise be eschewed as a source of supply, for its shingle looks entirely out of place among plants from the alps. The ground limestone and granite chips sold as chicken grit are excellent for surfacing pans and sinks, but rather too small for a larger area, besides which the former, being almost white in colour, tend to produce a somewhat artificial effect.

Before the war, many nurserymen used to supply chippings in several varieties, but I have not seen them advertised in any recent catalogues. A diligent search of the neighbouring quarries, therefore, seems to be the only practicable solution. Rather to my surprise, I found a good supply of limestone chips of suitable size and colour at a sandstone quarry in Surrey. They were, of course, imported from a limestone district, but despite this were not unduly expensive—for these days.

If the rocks used in the construction of the garden are sandstone the gardener has a more difficult quest, for both limestone and granite chippings will look hopelessly incongruous in such a setting and sandstone

chips of the requisite quality are very hard to come by. The first con-
signment I acquired proved to be much too soft, with the result that,
after a few heavy rains, the surface of my garden resembled a tapioca
pudding. More recently, I have found a supply of harder sandstone
chippings in a Sussex quarry, but it is desirable to obtain these in a larger
size than with limestone or granite, or they soon become amalgamated
with the soil. For the sake of appearance it is better that chippings of
any variety should not be too uniform in size, and a few rather larger
stones may be scattered here and there on the surface with good effect.
An alternative for those who cannot procure suitable sandstone chippings
would be to use small flat pieces of sandstone, many of which will be
found to have detached themselves from the larger rocks while these are
being moved into their places. Some care, however, would probably be
necessary to avoid the appearance of miniature crazy paving.

Of that curious material, tufa, I have had but little experience except
in sink gardens. It is found between beds of magnesian limestone, but
only in a few places in England, so that it is apt to be expensive. It is
so favourable to plant life that many alpines will thrive excellently if they
are merely thrust into the chinks and holes with which it abounds,
though unfortunately this also applies to moss, with which it rapidly
covers itself. Its debris, however, strikes me as having distinct possibilities as a form of surfacing material for the rock garden, so those who live
in tufa-producing districts might profitably make enquiries from their
neighbouring quarries.

CHAPTER FIVE

IN THE SHADOWS

F OR MANY YEARS I laboured under the impression, gained from the books, that one of the most important factors in the cultivation of alpine plants was sun—and lots of it. Every author whose works I consulted said the same thing. 'Choose a site enjoying the maximum possible amount of sunshine,' was the burden of their song. True, Farrer himself qualified his advice on the point by saying, 'If, however, the water supply be poor or precarious and the climate especially torrid, then the more delicate and capricious of the higher alpines may profitably be given a site ... where the sun falls for only half the day.' But it is with the general run of alpines rather than the delicate and capricious that I am chiefly concerned; and whose water supply is not 'poor and precarious' during the occasional torrid summer which visits these islands—just at the precise time that water is most sorely needed?

Having done all my gardening in Kent, Surrey and Sussex, I eventually began to suspect that this sunshine business had been overdone, at all events so far as the warm southern counties were concerned. It was therefore with some relief that I read in the *Bulletin of the Alpine Garden Society* a statement by a Swiss expert which seemed to confirm this view. This occurred in the report of a talk given by the famous alpinist, M. Amyon Correvon, to members of the Society on a visit to Wengen, in which the lecturer observed that most alpines, when grown 'in the plains' in England, appreciated some shade from trees or a hedge, though they should not, of course, be planted actually beneath the trees.

As all our English writers agree in saying that no trees or large shrubs should be allowed near the rock garden (one of them giving thirty yards as the very minimum distance) I felt it was a little difficult to reconcile M. Correvon's statement with the normal English practice, and turned back to my library for further enlightenment. It then appeared that it was chiefly the authors of the older school who were so insistent on the need for full sunshine, and that the moderns were prepared to make some concession in this respect. Their advice on the subject was not, however, particularly helpful.

Mr T. C. Mansfield, for instance, in his excellent book, *Alpines in Colour and Cultivation*, stoutly maintains that a northern slope, even when in full sun, receives less heat than its opposite number on the south side, owing to the different angle at which the solar rays strike the ground. From this he deduces that plants which do not appreciate too much baking should be planted on the north slopes of the rock garden. Well, he may be right: I confess that I am not of a sufficiently scientific turn of mind either to prove or disprove it: but while walking on the South Downs on a hot summer day, I cannot truthfully say that I feel any cooler or hotter on one side than on the other. Moreover, as he then proceeds to apply the same argument to rainfall, assuming the prevailing wind to be from the south-west, it appears that plants on the north slope receive less rain than those on the southern one, so that these two factors tend to cancel each other out.

A more recent book, *Commonsense Rock Gardening*, by that well-known plant hunter, Mr F. Kingdon-Ward, contains a whole chapter on the subject of shade. I pounced on this with avidity as soon as the book came into my possession, but it did not give me the information I wanted. True, he has some interesting things to say about shade in the rock garden, and his diagrams are as clear as the daylight I hoped he was going to tell me how to exclude; but after a promising start, he wanders away from the point, and finally returns to his advocacy of constructing the garden for the benefit of 'sun-bathers'. He does, however, tell us that a cliff some three feet high, facing north, will give us all the shade we need, and that when the noon sun at mid-summer in London is 75° above the horizon, a vertical north-facing cliff only two feet high will get no sunshine all day.

These statements set me to work with a ruler and protractor to find out what he omits to add; namely, how far this shade extends—a rather vital point. If my calculations are correct, the answer is nine inches for the three-foot cliff and only six inches for the two-footer. Now in the average rock garden of today (for we can safely omit from our calculations such gigantic Victorian creations as Friar Park), a three-foot cliff is a pretty high one, and there must be many of us who can boast no mountain rising more than two feet above the surrounding soil. For all practical purposes, therefore, we may assume that rocks alone will not provide the answer, except for plants in vertical crevices in the cliff face and those nestling actually at their feet on the northern side. Admittedly, these calculations are based on the altitude of the sun at noon in mid-summer, but this is just the time when shade is most desirable.

Before going further, I ought perhaps to qualify these remarks. An excess of hot sunshine can affect a plant in two ways: firstly, by drawing moisture from the soil and thus parching their roots, and secondly, by its direct action on the foliage. The former, certainly, can be mitigated by the use of rocks or flat stones laid over the roots. I remember being once given this tip by a nurseryman as an aid to success with *Lithospermum diffusum*, and there are quite a number of plants which enjoy having their toes in the shade and their heads in the sun. Others, too, will tolerate a hot position so long as they are given plenty of water, but neither rocks nor water provide the whole answer to the problem.

My own rock garden, although perhaps a rather extreme case, affords a good example of the kind of difficulties involved. It lies entirely on a slope facing south-east, and as the rocks are sandstone—which to look natural should not stand up above the soil—the whole area is in full sun all day long during the summer months. A few plants can obtain some slight protection by huddling beneath the northern face of a rock, but there are are not many such positions, and the shade at no time extends for more than a few inches. What I want is a broad valley where all except the most confirmed sun-addicts can flourish without being grilled to cinders. On the other hand, a deep shadow lasting all day would be equally bad: dappled shade is the ideal to be aimed at, and this is just what is so hard to achieve. In order to save the lives of my Asiatic gentians during a recent hot summer I constructed a portable frame of bamboos, which was placed over their heads during long sunny spells. This certainly had the desired effect, but it looked most unsightly and I sometimes forgot to replace it after it had been removed for the benefit of visitors.

The lath or bamboo frame, therefore, can only be regarded as an emergency measure rather than as a permanent solution of the shade problem. One possible answer lies in the planting of dwarf shrubs where shade is needed. In order to obtain benefit from them at once, however, it would be necessary to plant mature specimens, which might be difficult both to obtain and establish, besides being rather expensive. A further drawback to this plan would be that unless the shrubs were too large to be in scale with the alpines, they would only provide sufficient shade for those plants almost directly beneath and to the north of them. Nevertheless, it would be worth trying on a limited scale.

All things considered, the most practical solution seems to be that suggested by the words of M. Correvon, and, ignoring the warnings of English writers, to arrange matters so that the requisite shade is furnished by trees on the south side of the alpine garden. (A hedge can be ruled out, as it would need to be so close that its roots would rob the soil of moisture and sustenance). If you have such a screen already growing, it becomes a matter of finding a suitable site for the rock garden close enough to benefit from the shade, but without being so close as to suffer from drip and root interference. If, like me, your site is already fixed, and you have to plant your screen, I suggest that silver birches would be very satisfactory. Apart from their own beauty, both in summer and winter, they cast just that amount of dappled shade which is so desirable, and their root systems are less objectionable than most.

I happen to have some young silver birches growing where they are not wanted, and I have it in mind to move these to a position on the south side of my rock garden. But although specimens up to ten or twelve feet can be safely transplanted, the shadow cast by a tree of this size will only extend to within a few feet of the bole. Considerable patience will therefore be necessary before the alpines can benefit from them to any noticeable extent, unless I follow the advice of Mr Haworth-Booth relating to shrub gardens and plant a double belt, the nearer one to be cut down when the permanent trees are large enough to take over the shading duties.

Altogether, it seems to be a most difficult problem, and I cannot pretend that any of the solutions here offered are in any way ideal. But perhaps these random reflections will suggest to the ingenious-minded gardener some means of solving his own particular difficulties in this direction in his own way. At all events, they should serve to draw attention to an aspect of alpine gardening which has hitherto been almost entirely overlooked.

Aethionema 'Warley Rose'

Dryas octopetala

CHAPTER SIX

ALPINES OF CHARM AND DISTINCTION

I HAVE DEALT first with various points arising in the planning and construction of the rock garden because these must necessarily precede the actual planting, but it should not be forgotten that the rockwork is merely a frame designed to show off the plants to the best advantage. As with a ring or brooch, in which the setting, though it should be worthy of the gems, is secondary to them in importance, so in the alpine garden the plants themselves should be the main objective. The nurseries specializing in alpines list many hundred species and hybrids, all sounding so attractive that the gardener who is not yet familiar with their Latin names may well stand appalled by the prospect of choosing a few dozen best suited to his requirements. In this and the following chapters, therefore, I propose to describe some of those which have brought me the greatest pleasure and satisfaction.

In between the common run of rock plants grown in every garden and those rare and difficult alpines against which the specialists delight in pitting their wits, lies a wide range of alpine and subalpine plants which deserve to be much better known than they are at present. Although many of them combine great beauty with ease of cultivation, they seem to be ignored by the gardening public as a whole, who are apparently content to stick to the well-known favourites which everybody grows, and seldom venture off the beaten track. These everyday plants have their place, of course; they would not have become established favourites unless they had proved their worth; but even in the smallest garden there is room for experiment with a few untried plants, and if these sometimes end in disappointment, they also bring many pleasant surprises.

Among the many beautiful plants I have grown during the past twenty years it is not an easy task to select the best: some excel in the colour of their flowers, some in the beauty of their foliage, others in grace of form or neatness of habit. In the following list I am confining myself to those plants which are not only pleasing to the eye, but are easy to grow, not too expensive to buy, and readily obtainable from most alpine nurseries. To the expert, of course, they are all old friends, but I am not writing for the expert. It may, therefore, be as well to add that, unless otherwise stated, they will all be perfectly happy in the ordinary soil and conditions of the

23

properly constructed rock garden. For the sake of convenient reference I will deal with them in alphabetical order.

The hybrid aethionema, Warley Rose, is well known to all who attend the horticultural shows, but there are several wild species of aethionema which, if not quite so striking in the matter of colour, are to my mind still more attractive. Of these, the one most often found in catalogues is *A. pulchellum*, a robust and hearty creature of considerable charm, bearing in the summer months flattish heads of pale creamy pink flowers which contrast delightfully with the blue-grey foliage. With me it has proved a much better 'doer' than Warley Rose, and seeds itself so freely that I always have a plentiful reserve supply for myself and my friends. *A. grandiflorum* is to all intents and purposes a larger version of this, and *A. schistosum* is also well worth a place.

An unusual plant which always attracts the attention of my garden visitors is *Anacyclus atlanticus*, which looks like a floral catherine wheel. Its prostrate stems, clad in attractive feathery foliage, radiate from the centre so as to form a perfect circle of anything up to two feet in diameter, and in late spring the firework display begins with an eruption of brilliant scarlet buds, which finally burst into white stars, glowing red on their undersides. Although quite easy and hardy in a sunny, well-drained spot, it is one of those plants which appreciate some protection from the rains of winter. *A. depressus* is very similar, and both are admirable for a large pan in the cold greenhouse.

Asperula suberosa is probably better known than any of the other plants mentioned in this chapter, being a fairly regular visitor to the flower shows, but it looks so delicate that I fancy many people are frightened of it. In actual fact it is a perfectly sound perennial, its only fad being that, like the last-named plant, it likes to keep its head dry in winter. All through the summer months its silver-clad heralds flourish aloft their pink trumpets, creating a harmony no less pleasing because it is seen rather than heard. It should be given a choice place on a high ledge where its beauty can be appreciated without stooping, and it is an admirable plant for a sink or trough. *AA. hirta, lilacaeflora caespitosa* and *nitida* are also well worth growing, but they lack the peculiar charm of *A. suberosa*.

Centaurium scilloides, sometimes known as *Erythraea diffusa* or *E. Massonii*, is a cousin of the gentians, but with flowers of clear rose-pink. It is generally described as resembling a pink *Gentiana verna*, though in point of fact its small glossy leaves are more like those of *G. bavarica*. At all events it is a most attractive little plant in a quiet way, and should certainly find a place in the alpine meadow.

Codonopsis clematidea is perhaps not everybody's cup of tea, and some may even dislike it on account of its strangely pungent odour, somewhat reminiscent of foxes. The scent (in its hunting rather than boudoir significance) is, however, only produced when the plant is handled, and seems to emanate from the stems and roots rather than from the flowers. While potting a batch of codonopsis seedlings I have at times been almost overpowered by it but, once planted, if you leave the creature alone, it will not offend even the most sensitive nostrils. It is a close relation of the campanulas, and bears bell-shaped flowers of the palest blue imaginable, most surprisingly marked on the inside with vivid splashes of orange and maroon. Personally, I am very partial to it.

The name convolvulus sends a shudder through all right-minded gardeners, who are only too well acquainted with the two English representatives of the genus, known variously as bindweed, woodbine and—in Sussex—somewhat euphemistically as 'lilies'. As a matter of fact even these are so lovely that, if they were rare and finicky plants instead of being unmitigated garden pests, they would surely command a high price, but fortunately they have several foreign relations of equal beauty but more gentlemanly manners. *C. Cneorum*, a Spanish grandee with a name suggestive of adenoids, is generally held to be the most handsome, but as it is not entirely hardy I give pride of place to *C. mauritanicus* which, in the south of England, at all events, seems to survive our winters in safety. This is, indeed, a very lovely plant, covering itself with wide trumpets of clear lavender-blue from June until late autumn. My garden visitors, on hearing its name and noting the wide mats of grey-green foliage, throw up their hands in amazement at my temerity, but as a matter of fact it is perfectly safe, having none of the deplorably nomadic habits of its English relatives. It looks best when planted near the top of a dry wall or rocky bank, where it can cascade downwards for the beholder's delight and its own comfort.

One has only to mention geraniums to conjure up visions of prim Victorian flower beds in patriotic patterns of red, white and blue, but the plants thus used—or misused— by our grandsires should more properly be termed pelargoniums. The true geraniums, or cranesbills, are very different cattle, and indeed hardly recognizable as belonging to the same family. They are all perfectly hardy, and include a number of delightful plants both for the herbaceous border and the alpine garden, of which my favourite is the one chosen to bear the august name of Farrer himself. Although only a small plant, *G. Farreri* (sometimes known as *G. napuligerum*) bears relatively large flowers of clear apple-blossom pink offset by a central hub of black anthers, whose charm is still further accentuated by the attractively shaped leaves of bronze-green tinged with vermilion. I like to plant it freely among the gentians, campanulas, violas and other small fry of the alpine pastures, and as it is readily raised from seed, a plentiful supply is always assured. The only difficulty is to gather the seed at the psychological moment, for in common with all geraniums it is armed with an ingenious kind of catapult by means of which it playfully bombards its neighbours as soon as the seed is ripe. Many a time have I watched my plants of *G. Farreri* for a week or more and then, just as I judged that the harvest was ready, have arrived one morning to find it all scattered abroad. For some reason these self-sown seed never seem to germinate, but when sown by hand in a pot or pan the seedlings appear with the promptitude and profusion of mustard and cress.

Dr Houston, or whoever was responsible for naming *Houstonia coerulea*, must, I am afraid, have been carried away by his enthusiasm for this little plant, the colour of whose flowers cannot truthfully be said to match the pure azure of the sky. Nevertheless, if one can overlook this mild deception, it is easy enough to be captivated by 'Bluets', as the Americans call it. The small flowers of powder-blue with just a hint of lavender are borne in great numbers on thread-like stems above the minute green leaves, combining to produce an effect of airy grace which is irresistible. *H. coerulea* should never be planted on the arid slopes of the rock garden, but low down in the valley in a moist spot, preferably in semi-shade, where it will soon spread into a respectable, though never invasive, mat.

I can never understand why the lewisias are not more commonly grown. Those of the cotyledon fraternity are, it is true, so promiscuous in their habits that the plants one buys are almost certain to be variable hybrids, but they are all so attractive that this is of little moment. They are sturdy looking plants, bearing flowers in different combinations of salmon, pink and apricot above symmetrical rosettes of leaves resembling green leather. They like a sunny, well-drained position, but with plenty of water during the summer months.

L. rediviva is of quite different habit, having enormous, almost stem-less flowers which look as though they were made of pink tissue paper, and narrow squinny leaves which vanish completely as the blooms fade. For this reason it should be clearly marked with a label, or it may easily be uprooted in its dormant period by some over-zealous weeder. *L. rediviva* likes to be completely dry and sunbaked after flowering until the foliage reappears in late autumn, after which, unlike most of the inhabitants of the rock garden, it needs plenty of water throughout the winter. The loveliest of all the lewisias, *L. Tweedyi*, fails to qualify for this list on account of its exorbitant price and uncertain temperament.

Linum salsoloides is a white flax of prostrate habit and remarkable attraction, enjoying a similar situation to *Convolvulus mauritanicus*, for which it forms a good companion. It seems to be a very variable plant, and I have more than one form in my garden, the best being very good indeed. The flowers, which appear in June and July, are of the typical flax shape, and in colour a glistening white with faint pinkish-brown pencilling. The foliage, resembling prostrate grey-green mare's-tails, remains attractive throughout the summer.

The next plant on my list is one of my very special favourites: indeed, when it is seen in flower, it is hard to imagine anything lovelier. *Oxalis adenophylla*, of the same genus as our humble native wood sorrell, comes from the Andes, but makes itself perfectly at home in England, and is in fact one of the longest-lived of all alpines. It is a bulbous-rooted plant, forming cushions of blue-grey leaves, curiously pleated like a half-open fan, upon which the large flowers of satiny pink with crimson eyes perch like exotic butterflies. Its only fault is that its blooms need sunshine to make them open, and even on a sunny day are apt to take a siesta in the afternoon. *O. enneaphylla*, from the Falkland Islands, is a white-flowered beauty of equal merit and ease of cultivation.

Ramonda myconi (formerly known as *Ramondia pyrenaica*), though a fairly regular visitor at the shows, still seems to be a stranger to the average rock garden. It is happiest in a crevice between two rocks, preferably facing north but at all events in partial shade, and forms a handsome rosette of crinkly dark green leaves, from which, in early summer, spring several stout stems bearing large flowers of clear lilac with golden centres. The ramondas, of which there are several species, bear a superficial resemblance to primulas (which they were once believed to be) and are among the very few plants best increased by the curious method of leaf cuttings.

The common *Sisyrinchium bermudianun* is not unattractive as an edging, but its small blue flowers are too much overwhelmed by the profusion of its sword-like leaves to make it of any great account for the alpine garden proper. It has, however, a relative from British Columbia of outstanding distinction and startling beauty. This sisyrinchium, *S. grandiflorum* (or *Douglasii*) has tall foliage resembling a clump of rushes, from which large bells of vivid Tyrian purple burst forth upon the dark days of February with astonishing effect. The whole plant then disappears from human ken until the following winter, and, like *Lewisia rediviva*, should therefore be carefully marked. A leafy soil seems to suit it best, but although quite an easy and accommodating plant, it is very slow to increase—unlike its smaller relations, which are difficult to keep within reasonable bounds.

I end this chapter with two beautiful cousins of the campanulas, *Wahlenbergia pumilio* and *W. serpyllifolia*, one or both of which are sometimes found sheltering under the closely-allied genus of edraianthus. Both are so attractive that I can never quite make up my mind which is my favourite. Farrer seems to have encountered the same difficulty, for he described the former as 'The jewel of the family' and the latter as 'By far the most splendid of all'; a distinction, however, which conveys an adequate idea of their respective merits.

W. pumilio certainly gains the most marks for the attraction of its foliage, which takes the form of an enchanting little tuffet resembling a small grey hedgehog; but its lavender cups, though lovely enough against such a background, fall short of the imperial splendour of the other's violet bells, particularly in its *major* form. Unfortunately, however, the flowers of *W. serpyllifolia* are all too evanescent, yet such is their charm that it is worth waiting through 50 flowerless weeks for their brief fortnight's display in June.

I have, of course, only mentioned a few of the beautiful plants available to the modern alpine gardener, and I have not included those belonging to the larger genera and other special categories, which will be dealt with in later chapters. Individual tastes vary but I venture to say with some confidence that even a small selection of the alpines I have described will add that touch of beauty and distinction which is needed to lift the average rock garden out of the common rut.

CHAPTER SEVEN

TRUE BLUE

It is curious what a powerful fascination the colour blue seems to exercise over the minds of gardening enthusiasts, and I believe most nurserymen would agree that plants bearing blue flowers are in greater demand than those of any other colour. At all events, they are for ever trying to raise bluer and better versions of such things as irises, sweet peas and Michaelmas daisies, and if the resulting crop of 'Blue Gowns', 'Blue Ensigns' and 'Bluejackets' are little more than examples of wishful thinking, they certainly serve to show the trend of the public taste.

The fact is, that Nature herself employs blue very sparingly as a primary colour. Of reds and yellows there are plenty for the gardener to choose from, but flowers of pure, unadulterated blue, such as those of *Salvia patens*, for instance, are comparatively rare. Some years ago, when I owned a small alpine nursery, I was sometimes asked to recommend blue-flowered plants for the rock garden, and for the contents of the present chapter I have drawn on the notes I made at the time.

Opinions vary, of course, as to what actually constitutes 'blue', but there are a few flowers on which I fancy the verdict would be unanimous. These are the ones which incline to the green rather than the violet end of the spectrum. The gentians (which I shall deal with in greater detail in a subsequent chapter) at once occur to mind as examples, though by no means all of even the blue-flowered species entirely fulfil this requirement. But *GG. acaulis, verna, Farreri, sino-ornata* and hybrids between the last two possess claims which must surely be regarded as indisputable. They almost shout 'blue' at you.

Next to the gentians, I would place that curious plant, *Parochetus communis*. Its pea-shaped flowers, on opening, show a faint hint of yellow on the underside which emphasizes the purity of the blue, but they spoil the effect by fading into tones of opalescent mauve after a day or two. Nevertheless, it is a most attractive plant, though unhappily not entirely hardy.

There is a little-known but glorious Chilean bulb, *Tecophilaea cyanocrocus*, with flowers of a blue as pure as anything in nature, but unfortunately its comparative rarity and exorbitant price rules it out for the ordinary alpine garden. I once treated myself to the luxury of a single bulb, which I planted with all due reverence in a pan in the alpine house, but, alas, it failed to oblige me with its wonderful crocus-like flowers. Another blue rarity is *Corydalis cashmeriana*, but as I have never had the good fortune to see a living specimen I can only judge of its blueness from coloured photographs, which do not always tell the strict truth. It must, however, be a very lovely plant.

Slightly further down the scale come a number of gentians which, though blue enough for all practical purposes, yet contain just a sufficient hint of purple to mar their absolute purity of tone. Those of the *decumbens* and *septemfida* groups are typical examples, while the royal blue of the lovely *G. Veitchiorum* is definitely flushed with purple.

Next to the gentians, most of the blue-flowered plants for the alpine garden come under the large order *Boraginaceae*. Many of them possess flowers which, when fully expanded, are undeniably blue, but by some freak of nature the buds are almost invariably pink on the outside, which keeps them out of the highest class. The bluest of all are undoubtedly the lithospermums, of which *L. diffusum* (formerly *prostratum*) is the one most commonly grown. The old variety, Heavenly Blue, has been a favourite for a great many years, but I find the newer Grace Ward much easier to grow and more satisfactory in every way. It is indeed a grand plant, and flowers throughout the summer months.

All the plants I have so far mentioned have flowers of medium or dark blue, but there are several borages which extend the range into the paler shades. *Borago laxiflora* bears attractive flowers of clear azure, but is rather coarse in the leaf and seeds itself too freely to be admitted to the close companionship of choicer plants. *Eritrichium strictum* (which we are now told to call *Cynoglossum Wallichii*) is much more select, and would probably be more widely grown but for the terrifying reputation (in cultivation) of its famous brother, *E. nanum*, The King of the Alps. As a matter of fact the former is quite easy to grow, if somewhat impermanent, and its silver-grey foliage, devoid of the woolly covering which is perhaps the other's undoing, makes a most pleasant setting for the flowers, which resemble those of a pale blue forget-me-not. There is also a true alpine forget-me-not, *Myosotis rupicola*, of dwarfer habit and flowers of a brighter blue: an extremely attractive little plant, whose short life may sometimes be prolonged by starvation diet and perfect drainage.

Apart from the gentians and *Boraginaceae*, the alpine gardener has not a very wide choice of blue-flowered plants. No such list would be complete, of course, without reference to the popular *Meconopsis betonicifolia* (or *Baileyi*), the so-called blue poppy of Tibet. At its best, it bears flowers of the purest sky blue, though in some forms, or perhaps on some soils, it is all too apt to degenerate into mauve. Although a true alpine, it is, however, too tall for any but a large rock garden, and is better grown on the outskirts of a copse.

The name delphinium is generally associated with the tall and stately hybrids of the herbaceous border, but there are quite a number of comparatively dwarf species, of which *DD. sinense* and *tatsiense* are the ones most commonly offered in the catalogues. Both have flowers of a glorious blue (either dark or light, in the former), but I never think they look entirely at home in the rock garden, and prefer to grow them in the front row of the border. A much better plant for associating with alpines is our own native milkwort, *Polygala calcarea*, which forms small compact mats covered, in early summer, with flowers of brilliant blue. As its name implies, it is a glutton for chalk. Of the flaxes, *Linum alpinum* is the only blue-flowered species small enough for the average rock garden, but unfortunately its flowers are rather washy in colour compared with those of the taller *L. narbonnense*.

Gardeners on limy soil who are deprived of the delights of the autumn-flowering gentians, may find some consolation in *Ceratostigma plumbaginoides*. This is a most attractive plant, forming wide mats of bronze-green leaves flushed with red, which, in September, become covered with flowers of a deep, rich shade of blue. It flowers best in a dry, sunny autumn, and seems to hold a peculiar attraction for Painted Ladies. I hasten to add that I am referring to the migrant butterfly, *Vanessa cardui*, of which several specimens, perched on well-grown clump of the ceratostigma, form an unforgettable sight. *C. Willmottianum* is equally beautiful, but more properly belongs to the shrub garden. There is also a third species in cultivation, *C. Griffithii*, but I have not yet tried it myself.

This completes my list of true blues for the alpine garden, though there are plenty of other plants—the veronicas, for instance—which hover on the borderline. But, as I have said, 'blue-worthiness' is largely a matter of individual opinion, and no doubt many gardeners would admit to the list plants which I have excluded.

I will end this chapter on a note of caution. The beginner, poring over his catalogues (and what a pleasant occupation it is during the winter months!) will come across a large number of plants described as having blue flowers, but there is a wide gulf between catalogue blue and the colour normally understood by this term. No campanula, for instance, should be so described by anyone who is not colour-blind. Another trap for the unwary lies in the specific name, *coerulea*. Many of the plants bearing this name, such as deinanthe, houstonia and nierembergia, are admirable and delightful plants, but to label them 'blue' is to employ a euphemism which is entirely unwarranted by hard fact.

CHAPTER EIGHT

A SILVER LINING

AFTER READING THE morning papers it is sometimes difficult to believe in the truth of the old adage that every cloud has a silver lining, but the gardener is in the fortunate position of being able to create his own, without which the green clouds of foliage are apt to become a trifle monotonous. This has long been recognized in the herbaceous border, but so far as the rock garden is concerned it is a subject which has been somewhat neglected. Yet there are many excellent alpines and other dwarf plants with silver leaves well suited to the rock garden, which, no less than the border, may suffer from a surfeit of green.

In compiling the list which follows, my chief difficulty has been to decide which plants may fairly be included in this category, for there are many with what is termed glaucous foliage which occupy an intermediate place. But although these have their value in relieving a monotonous expanse of green, I am confining myself as far as possible to plants whose leaves are of genuine silver, or silver-grey, unrelieved by any other colour.

I will deal first with the so-called carpeting plants, which may be used either as bulb cover in the rock garden proper or in the interstices of a paved path or terrace. Of these there are only a few with silver foliage. The genus antennaria furnishes several examples, and although rather large and coarse in the leaf, they are useful for covering the ground in the outlying parts of the rock garden. *A. dioica rosea*, the species most commonly offered, forms widespread grey mats and bears fluffy pink flowers which somehow never quite seem to fulfil their promise. I have also grown *A. aprica*, with whitish flowers, and there are several others of a similar persuasion.

Paronychia nivea is a much dwarfer plant, whose silvery appearance is enhanced by the paper-white bracts which enclose the otherwise almost invisible flowers. But the best, and by far the most silvery of the carpeters is *Raoulia australis*, which has been aptly likened by Dr Sampson Clay to a coat of cracked aluminium paint. It is indeed a most admirable little plant, either for the stone sink or the rock garden, where it may safely be placed among the aristocrats. Personally, I prefer not to underplant it with bulbs, whose dying foliage spoils the symmetry of its closely-woven silver mats. It seems to have a distressing habit of going off colour at certain times of year, so that for the first few seasons after making its acquaintance I lived in perpetual fear of losing it, but I now know that it always recovers itself again. In summer it becomes covered with a powdering of microscopic yellow flowers, which, however, temporarily detract from, rather than add to, its appearance.

This completes my short list of silver carpeters. Of silver or grey-leaved plants of taller growth or tufted habit there are plenty to choose from, many of them having the added attraction of beautiful flowers, which is by no means always so with herbaceous border plants of this description. First-comer in the alphabet is *Achillea argentea*, whose sharply-toothed silver leaves and flat heads of pure white flowers form a delightful association. It is sometimes listed as *A. Clavennae*.

The common Alyssum (*A. saxatile*) looks pretty enough on a dry wall, but is too coarse to be admitted to the alpine garden, and is apt to form a harbourage for slugs, woodlice and other unpleasant creatures. Of the artemisias, so valuable in the herbaceous border, the majority of species are too large for our present purpose, though *A. lanata pedemontana* is perhaps admissible.

Passing over the ubiquitous *Cerastium tomentosum* (snow-in-summer) in discreet silence, I come next to the heronsbills and cranesbills. Of the former, there are several with grey or greyish foliage which just fail to qualify. I think, however, we may fairly include *Erodium chrysanthum*, with finely-divided grey leaves and flowers of pale sulphur yellow; a rather rare colour in the rock garden. It is one of those curious plants which the botanists term dioecious: that is to say, bearing male and female flowers on separate plants. If you want to save its seed, therefore, you must be sure to have at least one of each sex. The cranesbills have given us a still more attractive subject in *Geranium argenteum*; a truly charming little plant bearing large flowers of clear pink in June and July, and whose leaves are as silver as its name.

A few of the hybrid helianthemums have grey leaves, the pink-flowered *H. × rhodanthe carneum* being one of the best, but as with alyssum, I prefer to grow these in the dry wall, for which they are admirably suited. The next plant on my list, however, is ideal for the choicest part of the alpine garden. This is *Helichrysum marginatum*, a comparative newcomer from Basutoland, which rather to everyone's surprise has proved perfectly hardy in England. It forms relatively large cushions composed of tightly-packed rosettes of brilliant silver, surmounted in summer by crimson buds which open out into white daisies. In its native haunts it must be a truly wonderful spectacle, but over here it seems rather chary of producing its flowers. Even so, it more than earns its keep on the strength of its cushions alone, and when these are spangled by the dew of a late summer morning there are few more attractive sights in the alpine garden.

If you asked someone with no knowledge of flowers to name a typical alpine plant, the reply would almost certainly be, 'Edelweiss'. Why this extremely common and not especially beautiful species should have received such wide publicity it is hard to say, but despite Farrer's exposure of the fraud many years ago, it continues to be surrounded by an aura of mystery to this day. Nevertheless, *Leontopodium alpinum*, to give the plant its proper name, has a definite decorative value in the alpine meadow when grown in the company of such things as *Aster alpinus* and *Dianthus alpinus*, for whose purple and rosy discs respectively its pale grey woolly leaves and star-shaped white flowers make an excellent foil. For those who prefer something more out of the ordinary there is a Tibetan species, *L. haplophylloides* (or *aloysiodorum*), which although taller and less silvery in appearance has the unusual advantage of possessing a delicious scent of lemon verbena.

Lupinus ornatus, from California, is a plant of such outstanding beauty that I can never understand why it is so seldom seen in gardens. In appearance it is virtually a miniature edition of the ordinary border lupin, except that its leaves remain more or less prostrate and instead of being green are of the purest silver imaginable. The flowers, which are borne on nine-inch spikes in June, are of typical lupin shape and soft blue in colour. It needs a certain amount of lateral space, as a good specimen in my garden measured two feet across last summer, but it is worth every inch of it and more. But if your rock garden really is too small, I implore you to find a place for this lovely little lupin in front of the herbaceous border.

Some (but by no means all) of the silver saxifrages live up to their name sufficiently to be included in this list, but as I shall deal with these at some length in the next chapter, they need no more than a passing mention here. For a bold effect, *Thymus citriodorus argenteus* is a useful little shrub, eventually reaching nearly a foot in height and twice as much across. Seen at close quarters, the small leaves are really a greenish-grey with cream margins, but the general effect at a little distance is of a soft, silver-grey bush. It has the further attractions of a pleasant aromatic scent and masses of lilac-pink flowers in the summer. The best variety is that known as Silver Queen.

I end with the common but pleasing *Veronica incana*, whose downy grey leaves make a pleasing contrast to the flowers of violet-blue. It is equally useful for the outlying parts of the rock garden or the front row of the herbaceous border.

All the plants I have mentioned are easily grown in ordinary light rock garden soil but, generally speaking, alpines with grey or silver foliage are more susceptible than the green-leaved species to the effects of winter rain and damp fogs, and this applies with particular force to those which are covered with soft down. It is, therefore, wise to take adequate precautions for their protection from October to March; a subject on which I shall have more to say in the chapter on the care and maintenance of the rock garden. For this small trouble they will amply repay you with the added brilliance of their silver when the spring sunshine calls them once more from their winter sleep.

CHAPTER NINE

THE BACKBONE OF THE ROCK GARDEN

THE PLANTS I have described hitherto belong for the most part to relatively small genera, but there are a few families of such magnitude that they demand separate chapters to themselves. Of these, the largest, numerically speaking, is the house of saxifrage, referred to by Farrer as 'the backbone of the rock garden'. So vast and so typically alpine is this genus that quite a sizable rock garden could be devoted to saxifrages alone, while a whole book rather than a single chapter would be required to deal with them in detail. Fortunately, however, only three of the many groups into which they have been divided are of real interest to the average practical gardener: the rest, with one or two exceptions, we may safely leave to the botanists.

The best-known of these are the mossy saxifrages, known to science as the Dactyloides section, of which nearly every garden contains a few representatives, though not always in their most attractive forms. The common variety with large off-white flowers makes quite a pleasing spectacle in May, but is not to be compared with the beauties which our hybridists have now made available. Most of these have their origin in the large and rather indeterminate group, *S. decipiens*, and their names and descriptions are to be found in every catalogue. The reds, in my opinion, are the most attractive, and although new ones appear every year the old *S. sanguinea superba*, which fully lives up to its name, is still as good as any. My own preference, however, is for the smaller and more compact varieties, of which Peter Pan and Pixie are as pretty a pair of dwarfs (in red and deep pink respectively) as one could wish for. Having a strong partiality for that rather rare colour in gardens, pale sulphur-yellow, I also like the hybrid Flowers-of-Sulphur, though it is unfortunately neither so free-growing nor so free-flowering as most of its kind.

The mossy saxifrages flower in May and are extremely easy to grow in any soil or situation, though if a choice is available it is best to plant them in part shade, or their blooms may become scorched by the sun and lose their bright colours. They are admirable plants for the paved terrace, the dry wall, the low-lying parts of the rock garden, or even as an edging to a path, and their emerald-green mats remain attractive all the year round.

The next section consists of the silver, or encrusted, saxifrages, known botanically by the uncomfortable name, Euaizoonia. This group includes some half-a-dozen different species and such a vast number of sub-species, garden forms and hybrids that it is easy to become lost in the maze of their names. They are, perhaps, the most useful of the saxifrages for all-round purposes, as they range in size from pigmies with stems of only two or three inches up to regal-looking plants whose plumes rise to as many feet.

In appearance they are quite unlike the mossies, and only the shape of the individual flowers proclaims their relationship. In this section, how-ever, they are borne in sprays and are for the most part white, with or without red markings. Their graceful plumes make a brave show in June, but even if they never flowered at all they would be worth growing for the sake of their shapely rosettes of grey or green, profusely spangled with beads of pure silver.

The species of chief interest to the rock gardener are *SS. aizoon, coch-learis, cotyledon, lingulata* (more recently known as *callosa*) and *longifolia*. Among the many different forms available it is difficult to choose the best, but I should be quite happy with the following: *SS. aizoon rosea* (pink flowers and red-flushed rosettes), and × Esther (creamy yellow); *S. coch-learis* (white); *S. cotyledon caterhamensis* (white with red spots); *S. lingu-lata lantoscana* (white); and *S. longifolia* × Tumbling Waters (white). The last-named is a truly noble plant; a natural hybrid between *SS. longifolia* and *lingulata*, which was first found by Captain B. H. B. Symons-Jeune growing in the mountains near Mentone. It has inherited the best features of both its parents, combining the size of *S. longifolia* with the grace of *S. lingulata*. It also has the great advantage of forming offsets, so that, unlike the monocarpic *S. longifolia*, the whole plant does not perish after the first glorious display. Like this parent, however, it takes several years to flower, during which time its rosettes, which are remarkable for their symmetry, continue to wax in size until in some specimens they are almost as large as soup plates.

The silver saxifrages are just as easy to grow as the mossy kinds, though for choice they prefer a light, open soil with plenty of lime. With the exception of *S. lingulata*, they give of their best in full sun, though they are as accommodating in this as in every other respect. They are, indeed, virtually indestructible, which makes them ideal plants for those who can-not afford to spend much time in fussing over their rock gardens. I like to grow them in dry walls and in the crevices between rocks, where their rosettes, spreading in a vertical plane, show themselves off to the best advantage.

Lewisia Howellii

Polygala Chamaebuxus

I now come to the least-known but by far the most attractive of all the garden saxifrages; those of the Kabschia section. Every real alpine enthusiast grows and cherishes them, but for some reason they are seldom seen in the average garden. Maybe the name puts people off, or perhaps there is a prevalent idea that they are difficult to grow. If the name is the stumbling block, they will not resent being referred to as cushion saxifrages, while the notion that they are pernickety may be dismissed at once as another gardening myth. To obtain the best results they need a little— but only a little—more care than the other saxifrages, and they are worth every bit of it.

The Kabschias form tight little hummocks of grey or green composed of many individual rosettes, a good deal smaller and more compact than those of most of the silver saxifrages. The flowers are of the typical shape of the genus but are borne on very short stems and show a greater diversity of colour than those of other sections. One of their great attractions is their early flowering season, which extends from February to April, just when their cheerful faces are most welcome. To me, the first flowers of the Kabschia saxifrages, hinting—even though sometimes prematurely—that spring is at hand, are one of the most heartening sights of the gardening year.

Most forms of these saxifrages grown in our gardens are hybrids, and their name is legion. In giving a short list of my own favourites I am not suggesting that there are not others quite as good, or perhaps better, for I have not tried more than a fraction of their number. *S. Burseriana* Gloria is an excellent white with exceptionally large flowers; *SS.* × *Jenkinsae* and Cranbourne, two good pinks; Grace Farwell, carmine; Iris Pritchard, apricot; and Faldonside, a superb sulphur-yellow with very grey rosettes.

They vary a good deal in their freedom of flowering, and in this important respect I have no hesitation in awarding the prize to *S.* × *Jenkinsae*. As I write these words in mid-February I have some small plants of all those I have named growing in pots on my windowsill. The generous Jenkins has—wait a moment while I count them—he has no less than fifty-eight blooms, not including buds, on a cushion only three inches in diameter; as many as all the rest put together. Last spring I had a dozen of him in my window and a lovely show they made, but I have since planted out all but this one in the open garden.

I have said that the Kabschias are easy to grow and so they are, though they amply repay a little extra trouble at planting time. What they appreciate best is a light, gritty soil with a liberal helping of limestone chips (the kind sold for tuning up chickens' gizzards suits them admirably), and, of course, perfect drainage. In very hot situations they are apt to wilt and die, so unless you are prepared to keep them constantly watered during dry spells it is desirable to choose a place for them which is shaded from the noonday sun.

As they spread but slowly and never grow very large, they should be planted where there is no danger of their being overrun by more rampageous neighbours. Being of dwarf stature, moreover (an inch or two at the most), they look best high up on the rockwork, as near as possible to eye level. They are also admirable plants for sinks and alpine pans, but I shall say more of this in later chapters.

Outside these three groups there are few saxifrages of garden value. Those of the Engleria section, which are to be seen at the alpine shows, are somewhat akin to the Kabschias, but much less attractive. To my mind, in fact, they appear rather grotesque, and even slightly sinister. A much better garden plant is to be found in our native *S. oppositifolia*, and many gardeners entertain a saxifrage unawares in their edgings of London's Pride (*S. umbrosa*), but this virtually exhausts the list.

Saxifrages are quite easy to propagate, but as the entire genus are of deplorably easy virtue it is no use expecting them to come true from seed, unless you are prepared to go to the trouble of enclosing their flower heads in muslin bags. The usual method of increasing them, therefore, is by means of offsets stuck into sand and treated as cuttings. This presents no difficulties except in the case of the Kabschias, whose rosettes are so small that masculine fingers seem far too large and clumsy to cope with them. With patience, however, it can be accomplished, and patience will again be required while waiting for them to reach flowering size, for they are very slow starters. It is therefore really better for the average gardener to buy all the Kabschias he wants, unless he enjoys propagating for its own sake.

CHAPTER TEN

JESTING WITH GENTIANS

'TO PLEASE PRIMULA is possible, to cope with Campanula is even comfortable; but there is no jesting with a Gentian . . . ' Nearly forty years have passed since Reginald Farrer wrote these words, and we are now on more familiar, if not actually jocular, terms with the gentian family. No longer need we approach them, unless it be in homage to their beauty, with the reverential awe of our fathers and grandfathers; for not only have we had a good deal more experience of the lovely autumn-flowering Asiatics, but, as Dr Sampson Clay observed in his book, *The Present-day Rock Garden*, in 1937, even *G. verna* seems to have lost its terrors.

Yet old beliefs die hard, and today I still find visitors staring round-eyed at the gentians in my alpine garden as though they were the flora of some other planet. And when I confess to growing some 25 different varieties, I sometimes catch a startled look implying that I must be in league with the powers of darkness. 'Much too difficult for me', is the almost invariable reply to my suggestion that the beholders should try some for themselves.

Well, of course, there *are* difficult gentians, just as there are difficult members of every family, whether vegetable, animal or even human. But as there are nearly a thousand different species of gentians scattered over every continent, ranging in height from an inch or so to over five feet, in colour through almost every shade of the spectrum, and in flowering season from spring until late autumn, such a sweeping accusation is manifestly absurd. As for such questions as 'Do gentians like lime?' this is akin to asking, 'Do gentlemen prefer blondes?' Some do, and some don't.

At the present time only a fraction of the known species, together with a certain number of hybrids, are available to the gardening public, and these are mostly the easier ones. Some, indeed, are no more difficult to grow than nasturtiums, while all will flourish with far less trouble than thousands of gardeners cheerfully expend upon those mop-headed mons-trosities masquerading under the name of chrysanthemum. Mercifully the gentian has so far escaped the perverting hand of the exhibitor, so that we have been spared the horror of blue floral gramophone trumpets.

From the viewpoint of the practical gardener, gentians may be divided broadly, if unscientifically, into four main groups: the European species,

flowering in spring and early summer; two groups, from the near and far
east respectively, blooming in July; and finally, the beautiful Chinese and
Tibetan species and their hybrids which carry on the display into the
mists of autumn.

Of the Europeans, only two are commonly grown: *G. acaulis* (in its
various forms) and the well-beloved spring gentian, *G. verna*, which may
be found growing wild in our own islands by those who know where to
seek it. *G. acaulis*, as everyone knows, is perfectly easy to grow, but extremely fickle in flowering. Innumerable recipes have been given for it,
but as the treatment which proves successful in one man's garden will
probably fail in that of his next-door neighbour, no useful purpose would
be served by repeating them here. An acquaintance of mine, after waltzing
her plants of *G. acaulis* all over her garden without success, finally thrust
them with a gesture of despair into a gravel path, where they immediately
burst into a riot of bloom. But it is not to be inferred from this that they
would do likewise either in your path or in mine.

G. verna is perhaps the only plant capable of causing the modern
maiden to become all dewy-eyed, and even strong men have been known
to exhibit traces of emotion when beholding it in flower for the first time.
Farrer's prescription was a sunny aspect, a porous soil with plenty of sand
and leaf-mould, perfect drainage, an underground water supply, and a
covering of glass in winter. All of which sounds very complicated, but as
I have said, *G. verna* seems more amenable nowadays, while for those who
still find it pernickety, there is ample compensation to be found in the
form known as *G. v. angulosa*. This is virtually a more robust version of
the type, and is, in fact, the form offered by most alpine nurserymen today. The remaining European gentians seldom find their way into post-
war catalogues, so if you covet them you will probably have to go, like
Mahomet, to the mountain.

In June there generally comes a short pause before the summer-
flowering gentians join the party. At the head of these I unhesitatingly
put *G. septemfida*, which is the ideal beginner's gentian and will flower
well in almost any soil or situation. With upstanding trumpets of soft but
rich blue, if not quite so spectacular as the spring and autumn bloomers,
it is an extremely attractive plant. *G. lagodechiana* is a dwarfer species of
the same persuasion, and *G. × hascombensis* a fine hybrid.

Of very different appearance but flowering at the same time, are the
cluster-headed species of the decumbens group. These form central rosettes of narrow, pointed leaves, from which spring several relatively long
stems bearing clusters of small flowers at their tips and at the leaf axils.

G. gracilipes, sometimes known as *Purdomii*, is the one most commonly seen, and has flowers of purplish blue. *G. Waltonii* is a shade darker and not quite so hardy, but the pick of the litter is *G. Kurroo*, a real beauty from Kashmir with much larger flowers of bright blue flecked with green and white. I have found it slightly more difficult to establish than the others, but once it gets going it seems as easy and hearty as the rest of its kind.

The month of August ushers in the third period of the gentian-lover's year. Everyone knows *G. sino-ornata*, but there are others of this group of at least equal merit, which for some obscure reason are seldom seen outside the gardens of the specialists. There is nothing particularly difficult about any of them except that, by and large, they cannot stand lime, though some are more tolerant than others in this respect. Even 'hard' water may prove fatal, so unless rain water is available it is advisable to put a pinch of Epsom salts into the can. They all like a light, spongy soil, such as a mixture of sand and peat, with good drainage and plenty of moisture during the summer. For this reason they do best in the north, but here in Sussex they thrive tolerably well on a slight slope in dappled shade, with short lengths of land drain thrust into the soil between them. These are kept topped up morning and evening in hot dry weather so as to get the moisture well down to their toes, for, like children, they prefer paddling to having their faces washed.

The earliest to flower is *G. hexaphylla*, a much smaller plant than the others, bearing attractive flowers of clear watery blue. Next, as a rule, comes the gentian which Farrer chose to bear his own name. No choice could have been better, for surely *G. Farreri* is the most beautiful gentian of all, if not actually the most breath-taking plant in cultivation. In a good form (for it is apt to vary) the colour of its trumpets is a pale blue of such startling brilliance that it must be seen to be believed. Yet close to it a plant of *G. Veitchiorum*, bearing flowers of deep royal blue flushed with purple, makes such a delightful contrast that it is hard to decide between them. Perhaps I am biased in favour of my Alma Mater, but I fancy an impartial umpire would give the verdict to Cambridge by a canvas.

G. sino-ornata, flowering rather later than the others, needs no bouquet, but *GG. ornata* and *ornata congestifolia*—two quite different plants despite their similarity of name—deserve to be more widely grown. The latter is the easier to manage of the two. Almost every conceivable hybrid has been produced between all these autumn-flowering gentians. Their names will be found in the catalogues, and most of them are well worth growing. Not that they are lovelier than their parents—that would be scarcely possible—but some, such as *G.* ×*stevenagensis*, are apt to be more vigorous and more liberal with their flowers.

Contrary to popular belief, gentians are quite easy to propagate. The spring and summer flowering species come readily from seed, *so long as it is sown as soon as ripe*, and begin to flower in their second season. Those of the *sino-ornata* group seldom set seed in this country without assistance, but they are the easiest possible plants to divide. You have only to dig up a clump in March, when, like the best Crown Derby in the days of kitchen-maids, it will come to pieces in your hands.

There are, of course, many other gentians cultivated by the specialists, and even my own very modest alpine garden contains several I have not mentioned. I have, however, named most of those commonly offered by nurserymen, and a selection of even a few of these, suited to your soil, will, I am convinced, give more lasting pleasure than any other single genus of plants, and with the minimum of trouble. Beginning in April, except for a slight falling off in June, there is hardly a dull moment till November, after which we must be content to dream our dreams until the spring sunshine brings *G. acaulis* into bloom once more. And, glory be, it is April again as I write these lines.

CHAPTER ELEVEN

COPING WITH CAMPANULAS

EXCEPT FOR A FEW queasy customers which seldom find their way into the nursery catalogues, campanulas are amongst the easiest of all alpine plants to cope with. They have an important part to play in the rock garden, moreover, by furnishing it with much-needed colour in those rather difficult midsummer months when there is apt to be a hiatus in the floral display provided by other genera. Their one drawback is a certain sameness in the matter of colour, though to compensate for this their flowers assume a variety of shapes—for by no means all the campanulas live up to their name in this respect. Some assume the form of stars, and others of cups, saucers, bottles, tubes and various miscellaneous vessels not usually associated with belfries.

Of the true alpine bellflowers, the best-known are the common but delightful 'Fairies' Thimbles', of which there are several named forms. The type plant has been the subject of considerable confusion, having been known at various times as *C. Bellardii*, *C. cochlearifolia* and *C. pusilla*, and it may still be found listed under any of these names. Although it is attractive enough in itself, the best effect is obtained by planting a carpet of several varieties, such as Miss Willmott (pale lavender), Oakington Blue (violet-blue) and Farrer's beautiful find, Miranda, with tubby little bells of the palest shade of silvery blue imaginable. There is also a pleasant albino, which should be planted here and there among the rest in the valley or alpine meadow. They are all very free growers, but never so invasive as to become a nuisance.

The attractions of this little group will be still further enhanced by the addition of a few plants of *C. pulla*, a miniature bellflower to which I am particularly addicted. Its bells are much the same size and shape as the others, but in colour a rich, glistening purple of a darker shade than any other flower I know. They form a delightful contrast to the paler bells of *C. pusilla* and its varieties, but care should be taken that *C. pulla* is not swamped by them, as it does not share their robust and hearty temperament. Not that it is by any means a weakling, as it was once thought to be, but it is merely of a more stay-at-home disposition than the others. In former days it was believed to dislike lime in any form, but this myth has long since been exploded, and it is perfectly happy in the same kind of soil that suits the rest of the campanulas.

C. muralis (which I prefer to its other somewhat ungainly name of *Portenschlagiana*) is seen in almost every garden, and is a most admirable species for a dry wall or stony slope. Its flowers of medium violet-blue are intermediate between the bell and star types, and are borne in incredible profusion from June until late autumn. Altogether, it is a most obliging plant, and will flourish in almost any soil or situation.

Two good hybrids with flowers of a similar shape are *C. × rotarvatica* and *C. × Stansfieldii*. The former is a cross between our native harebell (*C. rotundifolia*) and *C. arvatica*, a special treasure to which I shall refer again in a moment. Its lavender-blue bells are quite pleasing, but I prefer *C. × Stansfieldii*, a first-class hybrid with violet flowers and curious downy foliage. Like most plants of this description it does not care for our wet English winters, so that steps should be taken to provide it with an umbrella.

Of the star-shaped campanulas my favourite is undoubtedly *C. arvatica*, a perfectly prostrate plant which forms a carpet of minute green leaves and covers itself in July with small violet stars. This is the smallest campanula in cultivation, and the only one I am prepared to admit to the stone sink, for which it is admirably suited. It should be planted in light, gritty soil in full sun and with perfect drainage beneath its feet. Like many of the campanulas, it also has a white form.

CC. garganica and *istriaca* are closely allied species with star-shaped flowers in varying shades of lavender-blue. There are several garden varieties of the former, some with hairy leaves and one, W. H. Payne, with white centres to the flowers, which add to its attraction. The flowers of *C. Poscharskyana* are somewhat similar, but this species should be avoided like the plague unless you have many square yards of waste ground which it is desired to cover as rapidly as possible. Unfortunately, perhaps, it is by no means unattractive when in flower, which must have led many people to plant it and then spend the rest of their lives wishing they hadn't. But possibly some may have been saved from this by the fear of being asked its name.

The flowers of all the foregoing campanulas are relatively small, but there are others bearing quite large cups, yet of sufficiently dwarf stature to be included in the rock garden. Everyone knows *C. carpatica*, of which there are many named forms ranging in colour from white to violet, all of them making a fine show in July and August. Yet somehow they seem to belong to the herbaceous border rather than the alpine garden, and I have even seen them used with excellent effect for carpeting rose beds. There is, however, a smaller form, *C. turbinata*, which I cheerfully admit to the select company of alpines. Most of the plants sent out under this name are probably dwarf varieties of *C. carpatica*, but I know of one nursery-man, at least, who claims to grow the true species. I have an attractive form in my garden known as *C. turbinata pallida*, with wide saucers of the palest china-blue, but whether this is the true *turbinata* I am not prepared to say.

C. turbinata is possibly one of the parents of a hybrid of great beauty, *C. × pulloides*, whose other parent is certainly *C. pulla*. Its cups have the same colour and sheen as the bells of *C. pulla*, but the whole plant is considerably larger. There is an attractive garden form of this known as G. F. Wilson, with flowers of a slightly paler shade of violet.

The king of all the cup-bearers, however, is unquestionably *C. Raineri*; a real aristocrat among campanulas, and one of the few which are more at home among the rocks than in the alpine meadow. It should be planted in gritty, well-drained soil in a horizontal crevice, which it will soon fill with its grey-green hairy leaves, on which the relatively huge china-blue cups perch closely in glorious profusion. The wise reader, having noted my description of the foliage, will take the appropriate action in the winter.

My next plant, *C. Tommasiniana*, strikes out on a line of its own, by producing bells so long and narrow that they more nearly resemble tubes, slightly wider at the mouth. These are borne in sheaves on long, wiry stems above close tufts of narrow foliage, and the whole effect is remarkably pleasing. It does not spread underground like many campanulas, but stays in neat clumps. There is no difficulty about its cultivation, and although it is rather on the tall side—up to six or nine inches—it never looks out of place among the alpines.

There are, of course, many other campanulas, both species and hybrids, suited to the rock garden, but those I have described form, I think, a representative and easily grown selection. Species such as the lovely *C. Allionii*, the curious *C. excisa*, which looks as though somebody had attacked it with a paper punch, and the equally remarkable *C. Zoysii*, whose bells are gathered in at the mouth like the nether garments of early Victorian young ladies, are best left to the experts with their alpine houses and other special facilities. There are also a number of monocarpic species which few gardeners care to trouble about, though some, such as *C. Formanekiana*, are worth a place for the beauty of their symmetrical rosettes, which often persist for several years before the plants commit suicide by flowering.

The campanulas like a sunny position in light, gritty soil to which mortar rubble has been added, but most of them have no special fads and will put up with treatment which the more fastidious alpines would never tolerate. Their chief enemy is the slug, which is said to show a particular preference for *CC. Raineri* and *Zoysii*—doubtless because of their higher price.

Many of the campanulas are very easily increased by division, so long as this is carried out in spring, when they are starting into growth. If taken later, there is likely to be a high percentage of failures, and the survivors will make slower progress. In March or April, however, almost every little rooted piece of the mat-forming varieties, if kept for a while in a pot of sand and well watered, will go ahead with such vigour and promptitude that it soon forms a new plant ready to be put out in the open. Those which grow from a central rootstock cannot, of course, be treated in this way, but must be propagated by ordinary cuttings.

CHAPTER TWELVE

DABBLING WITH DIANTHUS

In order to complete Farrer's triad I ought now, of course, to set about pleasing primula, but the melancholy fact is—and I blush to confess it—that primula, as a rock garden plant, does not particularly please me. I like primulas in the abstract, and readily admit that most of them have a high garden value, but to me they seem to have a certain air of smugness and artificiality which unfits them for the society of other alpine plants. I must at once make this clear that this is a purely personal view, and I do not wish to discourage any of my readers from growing primulas in the rock garden. As a matter of fact I do grow a few myself, but they are among the very few alpines which I would rather see in pans than in the open ground. The tall Asiatic species of the candelabra and similar types are, of course, quite a different proposition and I am very fond of them, but, alas, they demand bog-garden conditions, with which I am unable to supply them.

Having thus unburdened my soul and risked the wrath which commonly descends upon small minorities rash enough to express their opinions, I will now console myself for what I may have lost amongst the primulas by dabbling with dianthus in print as I have so often done in practice. And what splendid plants they are for the rock garden! I know of no other genus—the gentians always excepted—which provides such a colourful display in their flowering season, while many of them possess foliage which remains attractive all the year round. Finally, most of the dianthus have the merit—strangely rare among alpine plants—of a delicious fragrance.

For practical purposes it will be convenient to divide the dianthus into two groups: the grey and the green-leaved species and their respective hybrids. The first group is typified by our old and well-loved native Cheddar Pink (*D. caesius*). If the truth be told, it is liable to take up rather more than its fair share of space in the small rock garden, but I have not the heart to exclude it on this score. I have recently gone over my own plants of this pink with a pair of shears, which revealed the decomposed remains of several alpine neighbours beneath the spreading grey mats, but I have forgiven it on account of the great pleasure it has brought me by its flowers, scent and foliage. I ought to have attended to it sooner, of course.

For the owner of the really small garden, however, its dwarfer variety, or sub-species, *D. arvernensis* is to be preferred. This is a very neat little plant, being in effect more a compact version of *D. caesius* and bearing its flowers in such astonishing profusion that, in June, they entirely obscure the foliage. Its hybrid, *D.* × la Bourbrille, has received much greater publicity, but although it is an admirable little plant, I do not consider it any improvement on the type. The flowers of both are brilliant rose-pink in colour, and there is now a white form of la Bourbrille.

There are many other grey-leaved hybrids of varied parentage and considerable merit, but the taller of these should be relegated to the flower border. My two favourites for the rock garden are *DD.* × Little Jock and Mars. Both have bright blue-grey leaves, the former bearing large pink flowers with dark eyes and the latter small double crimson flowers like a miniature carnation. Mars is now a universal favourite, and deservedly so, but unfortunately he is so far removed from god-like immortality that it is wise to take a few cuttings from him every year. Unlike the great majority of dianthus, he is reputed to do best on a rather rich diet, plentifully laced with leaf-mould.

There are a few species of dianthus whose leaves are intermediate between grey and green, but as these are of the same shape and texture as those of the true grey-leaved plants I include them under this heading. *D. haematocalyx* is of this type, forming spiny cushions above which the reddish-purple flowers, with blood-red calyces, are borne on rather long stems. It is not one of the more free-flowering dianthus, but is an attractive plant, especially in its more compact variety, *D. h. alpinus*, which is more desirable than the type. *D. brevicaulis* is somewhat similar, but with blunter leaves.

A few years ago I was walking round the rock garden at Wisley when my eye was arrested by a patch of colour so vivid that I hastened at once to the spot to discover its source. This was my first introduction to *D. simulans*, a species found in Bulgaria only some 20 years ago, and renowned, even among this free-flowering race, for the profusion of its blooms. I was so struck by this plant—whose leaves were entirely hidden beneath the mass of rosy flowers—that as soon as I reached home I searched through my books and catalogues for some description of it. Only Dr Sampson Clay mentioned it, and his brief '*D. simulans* also grows' was not very encouraging. It was not included in any of my catalogues, but a year later I managed to find a nurseryman who had a small

stock of it, and ordered a single plant—for it was then rather expensive.
Fearing to trust it to the hazards of the open garden, I planted it in a sink
where I keep a small collection of rather special dianthus, but unfortunately this incurred the severe displeasure of a bird (a thrush, I believe),
who promptly pulled it up. I at once replanted it, but on two subsequent
occasions the same thing happened, which so discouraged poor *D. simulans* that it has made very little progress and has not yet obliged me with
a single flower. However, it is still alive, so I live in hopes of seeing its
rosy beauty in my garden some day. It is now becoming better known and
is included in all the more recent books on alpines and in a few catalogues
as well. It is a plant which should most certainly be acquired, even though
its price is still rather more than the usual one-and-sixpence.

In the same sink in which this near-tragedy occurred I have, among
other things, five very small species of dianthus with grey or grey-green
leaves. These I believe to be *DD. Freynii, microlepis, minutiflorus, sub-
acaulis and strictus brachyanthus*, but as the names of these midgets have
been the subject of some confusion and overlapping, I am not prepared to
swear to their identities. The one I assume to be *D. Freynii* is the most
pleasing of these, forming a neat little grey tuffet covered with miniature
pink flowers rather late in the season. It always reminds me of a plant of
D. caesius looked at through the wrong end of a telescope. Two of the
others are rather similar, and the remaining two, which I believe to be
DD. minutiflorus and *strictus brachyanthus*, bear white and pink flowers
respectively on stems that appear too long for them, which renders
them slightly less attractive than the others. Nevertheless, all five are
good little plants for stone sinks, and those who favour this form of
alpine gardening would do well to acquire one or two of them.

This brings me to the green-leaved dianthus, among which are to be
found several treasures of the very highest order. Generally speaking,
they are much more liable to variation than the grey-leaved kinds, so that
it is advisable to pick your plants while they are flowering in the nursery
plunge-beds. *D. alpinus*, in its best forms, is surely one of the loveliest of
all the race with its tufts of rich green foliage and large rosy flowers, each
with a darker central zone. Unhappily it is not a very vigorous or long-
lived plant in gardens, and is liable to attacks by the carnation-fly and
other evils, so it is as well to keep a reserve supply going from cuttings.
D. alpinus is responsible for two beautiful hybrids; *D. × Boydii*, which
closely resembles this parent, and *D. × calalpinus*, of which the other
parent is the lovely but rather tricky *D. callizonus*.

Second only to *D. alpinus* in this class is *D. neglectus*, which always seems to me singularly ill-named, for the sheets of pure rose which it makes in the alps could hardly be overlooked or neglected. But perhaps the name can be ascribed to the fact that its tufts of narrow leaves so closely resemble tufts of grass, that it might easily pass unnoticed when out of flower. Indeed, I have more than once only just stopped myself in time from uprooting it while weeding the rock garden in the spring or autumn. *D. neglectus* is even more variable than *D. alpinus*, to which, in its best forms, it is only inferior in size of flower. As if to make up for this and press its claims to the highest honours, its petals are buff on their undersides, making, with the clear rose-pink of the uppers, a combination of singular charm. This is one of the very few dianthus found in lime-free soils, but in the garden it seems quite tolerant in this respect. It is generally believed to be the parent of *D. × Roysii*, an attractive hybrid, though to my mind no better than the best forms of the species.

The foregoing green-leaved dianthus are plants for a select spot in the alpine meadow in company with other choice and non-rampant species. For the dry wall or rocky bank where sheer masses of colour are required with the minimum of trouble, our native Maiden Pink (*D. deltoides*) and its kindred are hard to beat. Of *D. deltoides* itself there are several garden forms with more brilliantly coloured flowers than the type, Bowles's Variety, Wisley Variety (with bronze-purple leaves) and Brilliant being three of the best. There is also a delightful white form with a crimson zone in the centre.

Closely allied to these are the very similar *D. graniticus* and two dwarfer and more compact species, *DD. myrtinervis* and *parnassicus*. The two last-named should be given starvation diet or they will lose the neat habit of growth which is half their charm and makes them, under suitable conditions, small enough for stone sinks. They are so alike that there is no need to plant them both.

There remain to be mentioned a few miscellaneous species which do not quite fit into either of these groups. *D. Knappii*, the only yellow-flowered dianthus, would surely have achieved great popularity but for its unfortunate insistence on looking like a gawky, overgrown schoolboy at the most awkward age. Its flowers are a most attractive shade of clear yellow, but are borne on long naked stems above a squinny clump of sickly-looking foliage. Indeed, the whole plant presents the appearance of being on the point of death, which, if the truth be told, it generally is. If only some enterprising nurseryman could succeed in producing a more compact and permanent form of this dianthus he would deserve to make his fortune, but although many have tried, all attempts have so far ended in failure.

D. superbus, whose large lilac-pink flowers look as though they had been torn to shreds by the wind, should be planted in the dry wall, where it makes a pleasing contrast to the more formal-looking inhabitants. *DD. arenarius* and *squarrosus*, for a similar position, bear heavily-fringed flowers of white or pink, and both have a delicious scent. *D. versicolor* appeals to lovers of the curious by producing white flowers which gradually turn to a deep pink, so that by the end of a week or two the plant is covered with blooms of several different shades. Unfortunately it does not always survive the winter.

The recipe for practically all the dianthus is much the same as for the campanulas; a light, limy soil, with good drainage beneath their feet. They are easily propagated from cuttings—or, with the grey-leaved species, 'pipings'—struck either in spring or autumn. This is greatly preferable to raising them from seed, from which they can seldom be relied upon to come true.

Those who wish to delve more deeply into the cultivation of dianthus should possess themselves of a recent monograph on the genus: *The Dianthus*, by Mr Will Ingwersen, whose name is a sufficient guarantee of the excellence of its contents.

CHAPTER THIRTEEN

CALCIOPHOBIA

THE READER WILL have noticed that the great majority of the plants I have described in the foregoing chapters like a sprinkling of lime on their porridge, but most of them are of a tolerant, easy-going disposition and will not refuse sustenance where this flavouring is absent. The reverse of this proposition, however, does not hold good, for plants which flourish on acid soils are so thoroughly scared of lime in any form that they turn yellow in the face and expire at a mere whiff of the stuff.

The gardener who wants to grow both classes of plant, therefore, is thrice blessed if his soil is neutral, or even slightly acid; for while it is a very simple matter to add lime in one form or another, it is quite impossible to extract it. Nor is it of any avail, if your soil is limy, to excavate a pit, however deep, and to fill this up with a spongy mixture of peat or leaf-mould and sand. For a time the plants flourish and you think all is well, but with the advent of the winter rains the dreaded enemy inevitably infiltrates into the prohibited area, whose inhabitants promptly perish. You might just as well give them a dose of arsenic straight away and put them out of their misery.

The only practicable solution to the problem is to build up a raised bed of lime-free soil, preferably between large blocks of sandstone, though railway sleepers have been used as a last resort. By this means alone is it possible to grow lime-hating plants in a lime-ridden garden. Whether this is worth the trouble entailed will depend on how greatly you covet these plants. Personally, I think it is—anyhow on a small scale—for I could not bear to be without at least a few of the lovely autumn-flowering gentians, whose views on the subject of lime I have already mentioned in a previous chapter.

On lime-free soils, of course, these difficulties vanish, though if ground lime or mortar rubble has been added to any part of it a strip of neutral soil should be left between this area and the home of the peat-lovers. This should be, for choice, in the low-lying part of the garden and in semi-shade, for most of the plants which enjoy such conditions also like plenty of moisture during the summer and some shelter from the noonday sun. This does not, however, imply that they do not need good drainage.

Primula 'Linda Pope'

Silene acaulis

Of plants suitable for growing in what I shall refer to for the sake of convenience as the peat-bed (though leaf-mould will do as well for most of them, and it should contain a generous allowance of sharp sand) there is a wide choice. As I have already dealt in some detail with the Asiatic gentians, I need not refer to them again beyond saying that once they have got into your system they are harder to give up than smoking, yet productive of far more pleasure than tobacco. My views on primulas do not extend to the peat-bed, for here many of the beautiful Asiatics look thoroughly at home, and unless your garden is a very small one it will be worth including at least a few of those species which will flourish in something short of actual bog. I am afraid my hot Sussex garden is really too dry for them, but I have grown here *PP. alpicola violacea, burmanica, japonica, pulverulenta, secundiflora* and *sikkimensis* with moderate success.

I often wish that most of the meconopsids did not grow quite so tall, for this makes them difficult plants to place satisfactorily. Being true alpines, they look quite out of their element in the border, yet they are apt to dwarf the rest of the inhabitants of the alpine garden unless they can be kept at some distance apart. The outskirts of a woodland is the ideal place for them, but as few of us in these days are fortunate enough to possess even a copse in our gardens, they must be grown in association with the alpine garden or not at all. Yet they are so attractive that I do not like to be without one or two representatives of the genus, and by careful selection of species reasonably satisfactory compromise may be achieved.

M. betonicifolia, or *Baileyi*, the 'Blue Poppy of Tibet', has stolen all the thunder at the flower shows, which has resulted in the rest of its kindred being comparatively neglected. It is certainly a wonderful plant if you are lucky enough to get hold of a pure blue strain. Yet there are others at least equally lovely in their own way, many of which surpass the blue poppy in the matter of foliage. Of these, one of my favourites is *M. Dhwojii*, whose rather strange-looking name is attributable to a Nepalese officer, Major Lal Dhwoj, who first discovered the species. It makes quite remarkably attractive rosettes of curiously-notched leaves covered with silky golden hairs, and would be well worth growing for the beauty of these alone if it never flowered at all. As it is, the flowers themselves add to its attraction, being pale sulphur-yellow with orange anthers, and borne on stems no more than two feet in height, which is relatively short for a meconopsis.

M. integrifolia, the lampshade poppy, is about the same height or slightly less, and bears enormous cup-shaped flowers of lemon-yellow.

But perhaps the most beautiful of all is the harebell poppy, *M. quintup-linervia*, with nodding flowers of lavender-blue on stems little more than a foot tall. Unfortunately it is not very frequently met with in catalogues, so that when a kind friend sent me a plant from Farrer's own garden, I cherished it with especial care, keeping it in a pot until I judged that it was able to stand on its own feet in the peat-bed. Alas! after lingering rather unhappily through its first summer it departed hence and was seen no more. My wife, whose gardening methods are slapdash but remarkably successful, said it must have died of over-cosseting, and probably she was right as I believe there is really no particular difficulty attending the culture of this beautiful species.

I have grown several other meconopsids, but as these were as tall as the average man, they cannot be said to be suited to the proximity of the alpine garden. The one great drawback to the genus is that most of them are little more than biennials, but as their seed both sets and germinates quite readily, it is a simple matter to keep a reserve supply coming on every season. A notable exception is *M. quintuplinervia*, which is a genuine perennial, thereby adding to its already considerable attractions.

The peaty bed is also the best place for *Lithospermum diffusum*, though for choice this should be planted where its long trailing stems can cascade downwards over the rocks. For years I tried to grow the old Heavenly Blue without much success, but the arrival of a newcomer, Grace Ward, shortly before the war at once solved my problem. This has the same glorious blue flowers as the old favourite, but a much more hearty temperament, and is really one of the indispensables for the rock garden. It can tolerate a certain amount of lime so long as it has plenty of peat or leaf-mould as well.

Deinanthe coerulea, whose flowers are not so blue as its name would lead one to expect, is a plant of singular charm for the peat-bed, though it has the disadvantage of being rather rare and expensive. It has curious crinkly leaves and large waxy flowers of pale lavender-blue with prominent stamens, the whole effect being faintly reminiscent of a begonia. It has the useful property of flowering in August, when the alpine garden begins to look rather bare, and seems quite easy to grow though not as free with its flowers as I could wish.

Calceolarias are generally associated with the greenhouse, but there are several dwarf alpine species, mostly with yellow flowers, which do very well in the peaty bed. Of these I have so far grown only *CC. biflora* and *tenella*, but there are several others equally suitable and attractive. The aquilegias also seem to appreciate these conditions, though they cannot be classed amongst the actual lime-haters. There are a good many of them, all delightful, but a selection from the following will satisfy even the most fastidious taste: *AA. akitensis, pyrenaica* and *scopulorum* (all with blue flowers); *AA. discolor* and *saximontana* (blue and white); *A. flabellata nana alba* (pure white) and two curious species with flowers the colour of cocoa; *A. ecalcarata*, which lacks the usual spurs of its kind, and *A. viridiflora*, in which the cocoa is relieved by a touch of pale green. Unfortunately they are not very long-lived, and as they cannot be raised from cuttings and most of them are wildly promiscuous, the maintenance of reserve stocks entails more trouble than the average amateur can be expected to face.

The majority of real lime-haters are to be found among the flowering shrubs, most of which—both the full-sized species and their alpine counterparts—prefer a rich woodland type of soil containing plenty of humus. The largest and most rewarding genus is that which, for practical purposes, may be taken to include both rhododendron and azalea, and indeed a large peat-bed could be devoted to these alone with most pleasing effect. Of the true rhododendrons there are innumerable species well suited to the alpine garden, ranging in height from two or three inches to as many feet. Some are so small that it is hard to realize that they belong to the same family as the great forty foot trees represented by *R. Falconeri* and its kindred. The flowers of most of these miniatures incline to shades of mauve and purple, but there are also species with white, pink, red, crimson and yellow flowers, so that no one can complain of their lack of variety.

The dwarf evergreen azaleas, such as the Kurumés from Japan, are also excellent little shrubs for associating with alpines, and a year or so ago I planted quite a number of them among the Asiatic gentians in my own peat-bed. Even in this, their first summer, they made a most delightful show, and they will increase in size and beauty from year to year until they attain a height of two or three feet with a spread of rather more than this. As their rate of growth is relatively slow, they should be interplanted with peat-loving alpines, which are gradually removed to another part of the bed as the azaleas expand. They will stand more sun than the rhododendrons, and are therefore better suited to a rather hot, dry garden like my own here in Sussex.

A very dwarf peat-loving shrub of which I am particularly fond is *Polygala chamaebuxus*, especially in its form known as *grandiflora* or *purpurea*. Although belonging to the same genus, it bears little or no outward resemblance to our native milkwort, *P. calcarea*, which, as its name implies, is a confirmed lime-addict. *P. chamaebuxus* and its variety are neat little evergreen shrublets with leaves not unlike those of the azaleas and pea-shaped flowers, cream and yellow in one, rosy-purple and yellow in the other. They grow no more than three or four inches tall, and seem to be in bloom all the year round.

Another attractive little shrub is *Andromeda polifolia compacta*, some 6 inches in height and bearing flowers like pink lilies of the valley. This may safely be planted on the sunnier side of the peat-bed, and indeed it has done well here in full exposure. The cassiopes (named after the mother of Andromeda) have flowers of a similar shape, but pure white. I have not had much success with them so far, probably because they like cooler and shadier conditions than I am able to give them.

A number of small ericaceous shrubs belonging to various genera will be found in the catalogues of nurserymen specializing in such things, but the true heaths and heathers (erica and calluna) are, to my way of thinking, best kept away from the alpines and given a special part of the garden to themselves, where on suitable soils they can form a very attractive feature.

Most shrubs are quite easily propagated by means of cuttings or, with the prostrate kinds, by layering, though it is apt to be rather a slow process. But as they are much longer lived and less liable to casualties than the herbaceous alpines, there is no need for the amateur to concern himself with this, unless he merely wishes to increase his existing stock of plants.

CHAPTER FOURTEEN

DWARF CONIFERS

THERE ARE TWO schools of thought about dwarf conifers as suitable plants for the alpine garden. Some, such as Mr Kingdon-Ward, will not admit them at any price; others, among whom I include myself, welcome them with open arms as affording a most pleasant contrast, both in form and colour, to the alpine plants. I think the prejudice against them, where it exists, arises from their all-too frequent misuse. The sight of the popular 'Noah's Ark' juniper rearing its miniature spire from the topmost pinnacle of rock, where it could not possibly live in nature, is indeed enough to put anyone off dwarf conifers for ever. In their right places, however, they can enhance the general effect to a surprising degree by breaking up otherwise monotonous contours and helping to create the illusion—if this is what we are after—of a mountain-side in miniature.

It should be clearly understood that by dwarf conifers I do not mean those little stunted trees which have for centuries been so popular in Japan. These are full-sized trees which have been artificially dwarfed, poor things, by being kept root-pruned and permanently pot-bound; a process sometimes occupying several generations of the same family before the desired effect is eventually achieved. Such trees, if planted in the open garden, would of course revert to their normal habit. The true dwarfs, on the other hand, are mostly sports from ordinary trees, and provided that they are grown on their own roots (the usual practice in English nurseries, but by no means always true of imported specimens) they will retain their dwarf habit permanently.

There are now some hundreds of these little trees in cultivation, though only a relatively small proportion of them are raised commercially in this country. Their names—thanks largely to foreign growers—have been involved in considerable confusion, but nowadays the leading English raisers adopt as a basis the nomenclature of Murray Hornibrook, whose book, *Dwarf and Slow-growing Conifers*, is still regarded as the standard work on the subject today. Since Hornibrook wrote, however, many new varieties have been introduced and the different genera have become so minutely subdivided that many of the little trees bear names almost as long as themselves. This is a drawback of which anyone who attempts to write about them must be all-too conscious; so, lest I be accused of pedantry, I make haste to plead that I was not responsible for their naming.

Most of the dwarf conifers are extremely easy to grow and very accommodating in the matter of soil and situation. The junipers are by nature lime-lovers and some of the cypresses are said to prefer a lime-free soil, but personally I have never found any of them at all pernickety in this respect. Therefore, while it is always wise to pay attention to the likes and dislikes of any plant, we can afford, in this instance, to make appropriateness of position our primary consideration. I shall refer to this again when considering the individual species, but the following may be taken as a general guide to their placing. Trees of columnar or conical shape should be planted low down at the foot of the cliffs, and should never appear against the skyline. Those of prostrate, or semi-prostrate habit may occupy the highest summits of the rockwork, where in nature they would have been stunted by the winds sweeping across the heights. For the intermediate shoulders and ledges there are plenty of forms of varying shapes and sizes, some compact, others more spreading in habit. Finally there are species grown chiefly for the beauty of their foliage—which in some assumes remarkable colours—and these are best grown on the outskirts or approaches of the rock garden. The subject is one which has been strangely neglected by writers, a notable exception being Captain B. H. B. Symons-Jeune, who devoted two chapters of his book, *Natural Rock Gardening*, to a study of dwarf conifers and their correct positioning.

Of the dozen or so genera which have furnished us with dwarf forms, cypress and juniper possess the greatest number of varieties and are the most widely grown. The former genus is divided into four main groups, the best-known being derived from Lawson's cypress, so popular in Victorian days both as a lawn specimen and for hedging purposes.

The variety *Chamaecyparis Lawsoniana Fletcheri* has received a good deal of publicity, but it is now known to attain a considerably larger size than was believed on its first introduction and cannot be properly classed as a dwarf. In Mr Eric Parker's Surrey garden there is a specimen which has assumed almost the proportions of a forest tree, but although this is an exceptionally large one, *C. Fletcheri* may easily attain twelve or fifteen feet in the course of years, which puts it out of court for rock garden purposes. There is now a smaller form, *C. L. Fletcheri nana*, but I prefer the somewhat similar *C. L. Ellwoodii*, which has a more compact habit, a better shape, and a richer colour. Even this, however, will eventually reach a height of several feet, so that it would dwarf the rocks of all but a very large alpine garden; but as a specimen for a miniature lawn or grown as a pair flanking a flight of steps, its symmetrical spire of densely packed blue-green leaves makes it very attractive.

There are several smaller forms of *C. Lawsoniana*, of which the only one I have so far grown is *C. L. minima glauca*. This makes a broad, humpy bush rather than a tree, and is neither as small nor as glaucous as its name suggests, but is quite useful in outlying places where height is required to give emphasis to flat surroundings.

The *obtusa* group includes some much smaller specimens, admirably suited for rock garden work. *C. obtusa caespitosa* must surely be the smallest conifer in existence, making a minute, compact mound of bright green which does not look out of place even in a stone sink. *C. o. intermedia* is a slightly larger version of this, and there are several others of varying form and colour. The place for these midgets is on ledges and flats between the rocks along with the choicest alpines, but care should be taken to keep them away from the more rampant plants, which might easily swamp them, and from the taller kinds which would make them look ridiculous.

In the two foregoing groups the individual branches are flat and fan-shaped, but in the *pisifera* section they are much more densely packed with leaves and assume a cylindrical form. These little trees suffer even more than the rest from a superabundance of varietal epithets, a misfortune which reaches its climax in *Chamaecyparis pisifera plumosa aurea compacta Rogersii* whose printed name, if planted vertically in the ground, would probably overtop its owner. This should not, however, deter the gardener from planting this most attractive little bush, whose foliage has the merit of assuming a golden tint in the summer. *C.p. plumosa compressa* is rather similar but still smaller and more flat-topped, and there are others in both this and the *thyoides* section of which I cannot speak with first-hand knowledge.

Of the junipers, everyone knows *Juniperus communis compressa*, the Noah's Ark tree already mentioned, and nine out of ten plant it in the wrong place. It should always be placed as low down as possible, and looks well at the foot of a cliff if your rock garden boasts one high enough to be more or less in scale: otherwise it is better to keep it away from the close proximity of rocks. It is indeed a fascinating little tree and fully deserves its popularity, though perhaps this has tended to distract the public attention from other conifers equally good in their own different ways. It has also resulted in grafted specimens being sent over to this country in large numbers from the continent and offered at what is known as 'competitive prices'. Such trees, being grown on alien rootstock, are most unlikely to maintain their slow rate of growth and dwarf habit when planted out, as I know to my cost, having once, in an incautious moment, purchased one from an unreliable source. Within two or three years it had reached the same size as the largest genuine *J. communis compressa* I have ever seen; a beautifully-shaped specimen some two feet high which has been slowly maturing in a friend's garden for a great many seasons. Nowadays, however, all reputable English nurseries grow this and other dwarf conifers from cuttings, which, although slower in producing saleable plants—thereby making them more expensive—ensures the customer against subsequent disappointment. Would-be purchasers are, therefore, strongly advised to place their order with one of the well-known firms with a reputation to maintain, rather than to fall for a little tree in a box outside a florist's shop, however attractive it may be in appearance and price.

The Irish Juniper, *J. communis hibernica*, makes a tall, cylindrical tree reminiscent of Nelson's column, but eventually grows too large for the small garden except as a lawn specimen. There are, however, two prostrate forms of *J. communis* which are admirably suited for planting on the top of the rockwork. These are *J. c. horizontalis* and *J.c. prostrata*, which may possibly be synonyms for the same plant: at all events I do not know the difference between them, nor is this of any importance to the gardener. My largest specimen, planted from a 3-inch pot four or five years ago, now measures some three feet across, but is no more than the same number of inches in height, and its blue-green foliage has a pleasing habit of following the contours of the rocks.

J. squamata Meyeri is the bluest of all the dwarf conifers, but it usually spoils the effect by growing rather straggly, and in the course of years may become rather large for the small rock garden. Nevertheless, its colour is too attractive to be resisted, and as it is slow to increase in size, it will remain in scale with the alpines for a long time, after which it can be removed elsewhere. There are two further small groups of dwarf junipers typified by *JJ. sabina* and *virginiana*, of which I have had no personal experience.

The spruces are not as widely grown as they deserve to be, and even the specialist nurseries only list a few of the many known forms. Of these the best is *Picea Albertiana conica*, a delightful little Christmas tree from the Rocky Mountains, whose branches grow so close together that it appears like a solid cone of greenery. Personally, I like it better than *J. communis compressa* for a position low down in the rock garden, even though it may eventually outgrow its welcome. I also have a specimen of

P. excelsa Clanbrassiliana, a nice little tree, though lacking the perfect symmetry and dense growth of the last.

The thuyas are closely allied to the cypresses and, like them, are divided into four groups. *T. occidentalis* Rheingold is as golden as its name suggests (in the horticultural sense, at all events), but despite the attraction of its colour I prefer the better-shaped thuyas of the *orientalis* section. Of these, *T. orientalis Rosedalis compacta* is in the first flight of dwarf conifers with ornamental foliage. It forms a medium-sized bush, almost globular in shape, and obligingly changes colour three times a year, being yellow in spring, green in summer, and purple in autumn. Although perhaps a thought too artificial in appearance for close association with alpine plants, it is a beautiful plant for the outlying parts of the rock garden, where it always attracts the eye. There are one or two dwarf thuyas in the *dolobrata* and *plicata* sections, but these are not so good as the foregoing.

The cryptomerias, or Japanese cedars, are said to like moister conditions than other conifers, but the only one I have, *C. japonica Bundai-Sugi*, is doing very well indeed in my dry, sunbaked garden. In appearance it is something between a spruce and a juniper, and should be planted low down. Another good form is *C. Vilmoriniana*.

Other trees which have produced dwarf forms are the silver firs (abies), the pines (pinus), the yews (taxus) and the hemlock spruce (Tsuga), but as none of these are yet represented in my small collection I will pass on to my own very special favourite. This is a miniature cedar of Lebanon, *Cedrus libani* (or *libanitica*) Comte de Dijon. While the others are attractive in their own right, the appeal of the cedar is rather that of the Japanese dwarfs: it is a perfect replica, on a small scale, of a full-sized forest tree. Its only drawback is that it is still rather rare and expensive, but it is well worth every penny of the ten-and-sixpence you will probably have to pay for it—if you can find one at all. When I first obtained a specimen a few years ago I was foolish enough to plant it in a position fully exposed to the south-west, whereupon a gale immediately reduced it to little more than a bare stump. I was convinced that, as a tree, it was finished, but before going to the extravagance of buying another, I removed it to a pot in the cold greenhouse, and in the following spring, to my delight, it began to put forth fresh shoots, and by the following season no trace of its misfortune remained. It is now a beautiful little tree, standing in solitary state in a broad shallow valley with dwarf alpine plants carpeting the ground round its miniature bole.

Except for the cedar, all the conifers I have mentioned are fairly easy to raise from cuttings, preferably taken in June or July. Starting with a few different varieties, therefore, it is possible to achieve quite a respectable plantation within a relatively short time and at a reasonable cost. Some day, if I can find a suitable site, I mean to plant a miniature forest of them, which should make a most unusual and attractive feature of the garden.

CHAPTER FIFTEEN

CARE AND MAINTENANCE

THERE ARE FEW sorrier sights than a rock garden which has suffered from neglect: somehow it looks even more desolate than an untended bed or border, in which the weeds are smaller in proportion to the garden plants. In the rock garden, moreover, the more spreading species of alpines may themselves become weeds and will overrun and kill all their more stay-at-home neighbours if they are allowed to grow unchecked— as not a few enthusiasts must have discovered to their sorrow on returning from the wars. Even the rocks, deprived of their carefully-planned plant associations, seem to add to the general air of desolation.

Owing to the light, friable soil of which the alpine garden is—or ought to be—composed, the seeds of weeds germinate more readily here than in other parts of the garden, especially when they are afforded the extra protection of stone chippings. Ideally, weeding should be carried out at least once a month throughout the year and more often during the period of maximum growth, but this is a counsel of perfection which I confess I do not follow myself. It is a somewhat backbreaking task, for the ordinary garden fork cannot be used as in the herbaceous border and elsewhere. I use a rubber kneeler to save my knees and some very small implement—a kitchen fork makes an excellent tool—for prising up the weeds with the minimum of disturbance to the alpines.

Great care and some knowledge of alpines in all stages of growth are desirable when weeding the rock garden, for many of our cherished plants seed themselves, and it is only too easy to uproot the wheat with the tares and to cast both together into the oven, or compost heap. In time, however, one becomes able to recognise the various alpine seedlings, and if these are growing where they are required to fill gaps they can be left alone to develop. More often, they will be found either clustered together round the parent plant, or, with some species, scattered far and wide and encroaching on territory where they are not wanted. In such cases I pot them up to be grown on in the nursery bed and later planted out in the rock garden, the surplus being most useful either as Christmas presents or as a basis of exchange with one's gardening friends. But some alpines, such as the violas and erigerons, are so prolific that there is nothing for it but to harden one's heart and destroy them wholesale: in gardens, as in other places, it is possible to have too much of a good thing.

The same remarks apply to those rampant subjects which spread by means of underground runners. It seems a pity to curb the activities of a healthy plant just as it is getting into its stride, but if this is not done with the quick-spreading species the casualty list in their immediate neighbourhood will be a heavy one. I have only recently had an unfortunate illustration of this in my own alpine garden, where, owing to the pressure of other work, I foolishly gave a plant of *Dryas octopetala* its head for two whole seasons. It came to me as a small pot plant three years ago, and during its first summer looked so sickly that I doubted whether it would survive. Then it suddenly found its feet and spread like a forest fire, leaving death and destruction in its train. It looked so attractive with its masses of creamy flowers nestling against the dark green foliage like miniature oak leaves that I postponed its execution until too late. Now there is nothing for it but to dig it up and replant the whole of its valley over again.

There are other plants, of which aubrietia and helianthemum are the best-known examples, which, although growing from a central rootstock, spread too widely above ground for the comfort of their neighbours. These should be ruthlessly cut back with the shears in late summer or early autumn, and will be all the better for it the following season. If this precaution is neglected, not only do the adjacent plants suffer but they themselves soon become straggly and less floriferous.

Alpines are remarkably free from diseases, but like other plants they have their enemies in the animal kingdom. Chief of these is the ubiquitous slug, and I have not yet found an entirely efficient way of dealing with this revolting creature. My friends recommend various brands of slugicide, but the slugs in my garden must be of a specially tough breed, as they seem almost immune to all of them. Nevertheless, it is advisable to scatter little heaps of slug powder round the plants which form their favourite food, bearing in mind that they are thoroughly conversant with catalogue prices and invariably choose the most expensive kinds. As I mentioned in Chapter Four, stone chippings tend to discourage the more timid slugs in the same way as cinders, but neither of these can be relied upon to give protection. Some gardeners surround their special treasures with rings of zinc, which are said to be 100% effective, but I prefer to risk penetration by the enemy rather than turn my rock garden into a miniature Maginot line studded with metal ramparts.

The best way of dealing with the slug menace, if you have the energy and enthusiasm, is to sally forth after dark with an electric torch and collect the pests by hand. I used to do this in the days when I owned a small commercial nursery, but now that the financial motive is absent I fear I am too lazy to make more than a very occasional sortie when roused to frenzy by the disappearance of some special favourite, by which time, of course, it is too late. I once read in the *Bulletin of the Alpine Garden Society* that if there is one slug in the garden it will be found on *Raoulia lutescens*, if you grow this attractive little carpeter. I have certainly often seen their disgusting slimy trails on this plant, though they do not seem to devour the raoulia itself, but merely to use it as an assembly point or a stepping stone to higher things. It is therefore worth while paying an occasional nocturnal visit to *R. lutescens*, which acts as a useful indicator of the presence of slugs in the rock garden, and may yield quite a respectable bag without the necessity of searching further afield.

Birds are a great nuisance at certain times of year, and seem to take an evil delight in pulling clumps of mossy saxifrages to pieces. Whether they are in search of moisture or insects at the heart of the plants I do not know, but whatever the cause it is a most exasperating habit from the gardner's point of view. Nothing less than pure mischief, however, can account for their still more infuriating penchant for tearing strips out of the flowers of *Gentiana acaulis*. This happens every year, chiefly to the earliest blooms, and I know of no sight more calculated to arouse murderous thoughts in the gardener's breast than that of these glorious blue trumpets, for whose opening one has waited throughout the long, dark days of winter, lying in tattered fragments on the stones. It cannot be the brilliant colour alone which attracts these unwelcome attentions from the birds, as I have never known them touch the still brighter flowers of *G. verna* or any of the later-flowering species. I suspect sparrows of being the culprits, though as they seem to carry out their raids in the early mornings, I have never caught them red-handed, or rather, blue-beaked. But as I cannot bring myself to kill any birds, other than game-birds, I have to suffer their depredations with what fortitude I can muster and ward off their attentions as best I may with unsightly barriers of pea-guards until the mood has passed. Fortunately it seldom seems to last long.

Cats can be a serious menace in the alpine garden, and appear to be particularly attracted by peat. Although I should have little compunction in shooting these nauseating hypocrites, who prey not only on my plants but also on the birds which are so much more attractive than themselves, I am afraid this would not go down well with their misguided owners.

I have sometimes thought of planting a patch of catmint or valerian at a little distance from the rock garden in the hopes of distracting their attention from my alpines, but have been deterred by the fear of drawing still more of the brutes on to my premises. In the meantime, my Sealyham terrier—self-constituted curator of the garden—does his best to deal with them, but as he goes off duty at supper time he can make little impression on an enemy whose activities are largely nocturnal.

True alpines are, of course, the hardiest plants in the world, being accustomed to spend the whole winter in their native haunts beneath a thick blanket of snow, which keeps them perfectly dry. What they hate more than anything is the rain and clammy fogs of which our English winters so often chiefly consist, and one or two species cannot be grown at all in this country on that account. It is indeed surprising, when you come to think of it, that any of them survive at all under conditions so entirely foreign to them, and it speaks volumes for their wonderful adaptability that so many of them do so without any special precautions being taken.

As I have indicated in an earlier chapter, it is the plants with woolly or downy leaves (generally grey in colour) which suffer the most from winter rain, for their foliage collects every particle of moisture and is unable to throw it off as readily as the smooth-leaved species. For all of these a winter covering of glass is desirable, and for some it is essential. The single pane usually recommended is not much use, as it does not exclude driving rain or fog, besides being almost impossible to secure against being blown down by the wind. A small cloche is a much better proposition, but the joint along the top should be sealed with insulating tape to prevent the concentrated drip which would do more damage than if the plant were left unprotected.

Jam-jars are too top-heavy for the purpose, but shallow jars of the kind formerly used for potting tongues are ideal, if you can get them. I have not seen a new one since the war, but a few years ago I was lucky enough to strike a rich vein of old tongue-jars in a disused cellar beneath my house. How long they had lain there I do not know: perhaps ever since those happy days when Farrer wrote that enthusiasts had been known to exist throughout the entire summer on potted tongues and shrimps in order to provide winter protection for their plants of *Gentiana verna* (which, despite its glossy green leaves, likes to carry an umbrella from October to April). When jars are used, they should be slightly raised at one side by means of a stone, for alpines do not like to be hermetically sealed.

It is as well to take a walk round the alpine garden after a hard frost, which is apt to force some of its plants out of the ground. This applies particularly to primulas, which should therefore be looked over from time to time during a frosty spell. Those which show a tendency to jump out of bed should be carefully tucked between the sheets again, a little fresh soil being sprinkled round their crowns, and the stone chippings, if these are used, replaced on top.

Apart from these special circumstances, a top-dressing of light soil in the spring is appreciated by most alpines, and will help to promote their health and happiness. A useful compost for this purpose is a mixture of loam, sand and leaf-mould, with a sprinkling of crock grit for good measure. Old potting soil is also excellent for this. It should be worked well about their crowns, and with cushion-forming plants in which some of the foliage has turned brown—as sometimes happens with drabas and Kabschia saxifrages—the dead patches should be cut out with a sharp knife and the hole filled up with the compost. By the end of the season the scar will have been covered by fresh growth.

All this may sound as if the care of the alpine garden involves a good deal of trouble; more, perhaps, than most people can afford to devote to it in these busy times. Well, no worth while form of gardening—except possibly the culture of flowering shrubs—can be conducted from an arm-chair. Weeding is necessary whatever kind of plants you grow; annuals involve yearly sowing and planting and the tedious operation of pricking out; herbaceous border perennials, staking, tying and thinning; roses, pruning, spraying and manuring. As for pot-grown plants, such as chrysanthemums, why, the work of potting and repotting, feeding, pinching and disbudding seems never ending, and to judge by those of my acquaintances who indulge in these dubious delights, claims all the gardener's leisure hours. The suggestions contained in this chapter are in the nature of a counsel of perfection, and the general run of alpines will flourish with much less attention; some, indeed, with none at all, which is a good deal more than can be said for most of the plants we grow in our gardens.

CHAPTER SIXTEEN

A USEFUL ADJUNCT

ALTHOUGH, AS I have indicated in the previous chapter, alpines are the hardiest and healthiest of plants, a certain number of casualties are bound to occur from time to time, even in the most carefully tended rock gardens. Slugs, wet winters and accidents must inevitably take their toll each season, to say nothing of *anno Domini*; for alpines, though mostly perennial, are not immortal, and sometimes their allotted span is all too short. For this reason, if for no other, it is worth while raising a few plants every year, thereby building up a reserve stock to replace the dear departed.

Apart from this, however, there are a number of advantages to be derived from propagating one's own alpines. With nursery plants costing from one and sixpence apiece upwards, it is a by no means inexpensive business to stock a new rock garden of even moderate dimensions, but by starting with one or two plants of each of the species it is desired to grow and then increasing their numbers himself, the gardener can save a good deal of the initial outlay. Most keen gardeners, moreover, enjoy giving or exchanging plants with their friends, and a selection from one's surplus stock of alpines, neatly potted up and labelled, makes a most acceptable present which can be given at Christmas, or indeed at any other time of year. Finally, the propagation of alpines is a fascinating business in itself, and is one of the best ways of familiarizing the gardener with the various species and their individual tastes, thereby adding both to their subsequent well-being and his own interest in the rock garden.

There seems to be a fairly widespread idea that alpine plants are difficult to propagate or that it is a very slow process, but this is by no means true. To raise them on a large scale is, of course, a fairly formidable undertaking, but while the professional nurseryman thinks in terms of thousands or tens of thousands, a few hundred, or even a few dozen, will be ample to satisfy the needs of the average amateur. By starting with the easier kinds, even the gardener who has no previous experience of the work will achieve considerable success, which will spur him to tackle the more difficult subjects later on. As for the time factor, while it is true that a few plants make a high demand on one's patience, the great majority, if raised in the spring, can be planted out in the same season

Saxifraga oppositifolia

Gentiana Farreri

and will flower the following year. Some of the more vigorous kinds can even be put straight into the open ground without the intervention of a pot, and may flower in their first season.

It is not my intention to go into details of the various methods of propagation, which are the same for alpines as for any other plants. Most of my readers are presumably already acquainted with the general principles, for an interest in rock gardening does not, as a rule, come until the gardener has passed the novitiate stage. There are, however, one or two points which it may be as well to mention before I come to the actual layout and management of the small nursery which forms the chief subject of this chapter.

Alpines may be raised by any of the three most usual methods of propagation—seeds, cuttings and division—and with most species one of these methods is more suitable than the other two. We cannot, for instance, expect a hybrid to come true from seed, and often even the species will cross-pollinate if planted near others of the same genus. With these, therefore, it becomes necessary to resort to vegetative propagation, and whether this takes the form of division or cuttings will depend on the habit of the plant and the nature of its root system. These things can only be learned by observation and experience, though most reference books dealing with alpine plants give the beginner sufficient information to start him on his way. As a general guide, I have included a few notes in my earlier chapters on the best means of propagating alpines belonging to the larger genera.

The secret of success in raising alpine plants from seed is to sow the seed when it is absolutely fresh, though the need for this varies with different species. For this reason it is a great advantage to save seeds from your own or your friends' plants whenever possible. Several firms of alpine specialists now offer seed for sale during the winter, and this is normally sown under glass in early spring. Such seed, however, will necessarily have been stored for some little time, and while, often, this does not matter, seed from such things as gentians, primulas and lewisias sown under these conditions may take anything up to two years to germinate. Long before the time expires the gardener's patience will probably have become exhausted and the contents of the seed pan consigned to the rubbish heap. With these, therefore, if access to the plant is not already available, the best plan is to buy one and to gather and sow the seed as soon as it is ripe, irrespective of the time of year. If this is done, seed from even the slow-germinating species will generally appear within quite a short time.

Cuttings and divisions are managed in exactly the same way as those from border perennials, though, of course, everything is on a much smaller scale. In dealing with the small rosette-forming species the lady gardener has the advantage of the ham-fisted male, and indeed when 'making' cuttings of such miniatures as the Kabschia saxifrages and drabas, I have often sighed for the fingers of a fairy. But if neither ladies nor fairies are available to help, it can be accomplished with the aid of practice, patience and a very sharp razor-blade. Division is the easiest and most rapid method of propagation, and in some species the roots can be teased apart so as to form a number of small separate plants without the need for a surgical operation. The rooted fragments will often grow if they are planted out at once in the open garden, but except for the most robust growers I find it pays in the long run to keep them in pots until a fresh root system has become established.

Although it is possible to raise a few alpines with no more elaborate apparatus than a wooden box, a sheet of glass and a few flower pots, the gardener who intends to make a regular practice of propagation, even on a very small scale, will find it well worth while to instal a simple nursery layout. If he already possesses a potting shed, much time and trouble will be saved by choosing a site as close to this as possible, as the transportation of a number of small pots from one end of the garden to the other is apt to become a wearisome business and not infrequently results in their being overturned and their contents spilt.

At least one frame will be required, but two would be better and three ideal for the small nursery unit. One of these is used for raising seeds, another for cuttings and the third for hardening off. No greenhouse is needed, but if one is already available it may be used instead of a frame for the seed pans. Heat is quite unnecessary, and indeed even harmful, for alpines should never be 'coddled' at any stage of their existence.

Pots of 2¾ inches in diameter are suitable for the great majority of alpines, though it is better to use 'thumbs' (2½-inch) for the very small and slow-growing species and 'sixties' (3-inch) for the large and spreading kinds. For seed sowing, 6-inch pans will be found convenient, and either pots or pans may be used for striking cuttings. For carrying the pots from shed to frames an ordinary garden sieve is as good as anything, but it should be packed tight, or its contents will inevitably capsize.

All the equipment I have mentioned so far is the same as that needed for raising any kind of plants, but there is one most useful item in the alpine nursery which may be new to some of my readers; the plunge-bed. This is, in effect, a shallow trench filled with sand or some other porous material in which the potted plants are plunged up to their rims as soon as they have been hardened off, the object being to prevent them from drying out too quickly in the summer and to keep the roots cool. It also saves the pots from being cracked by frost in the winter.

There are various methods of constructing the plunge-bed, my own being made as follows. The soil is excavated from the chosen site to a depth of a few inches, and the sides of this depression are then lined either with bricks standing on their ends or with breeze-blocks. (Concrete would perhaps be better, but involves rather more trouble.) The effect of this is to raise the top half of the bed above the level of the surrounding soil, thereby assisting drainage. Over the bottom of the bed is spread a layer of clean clinkers or sharp rubble, and the remaining space is then filled up with sand, ashes or peat. Personally, I prefer sand, as being the cleanest to handle, but it should not be of the soft, binding variety, or it will cake like cement after frequent watering. There is no need to fill up the whole plunge-bed at the start, for reasons which will shortly become apparent.

The commercial nurseries, I understand, fill their plunge-beds as they go, first shovelling in a layer of sand or ashes, pressing a row of pots against this, and then adding more sand ready to receive the next row of pots. For the amateur, however, the method I use will be found much more convenient and the finished effect much neater and tidier. After filling, say, half the plunge-bed with sand, I level this off flush with the top of the bricks by running a short length of plank over it. The bed is then well watered through a rose, and the required number of holes for the first batch of pots made by thrusting a bulb-planting tool vertically into the sand. These tools are sold in various sizes, and the one chosen for the job should be slightly smaller in diameter than the pots. On withdrawal, the tool brings with it a divot of sand, which is tapped out into the empty part of the plunge-bed, until this eventually becomes filled with the excavated sand. The pots are then plunged up to their rims in the holes, and the same process is repeated for the next row.

The plunge-bed may, of course, be of any length desired, but should not be more than three feet wide, or it will be difficult to reach the pots in the middle of the rows. (If there is only access to one side, a width of two feet six inches will be sufficient.) It is astonishing how many alpine pots can be accommodated in quite a small space. A plunge-bed measuring twelve feet by three feet will hold 500 2¾-inch pots if the rows are staggered, and this should more than suffice for the requirements of the average amateur. Some years ago I had a small commercial nursery with twenty plunge-beds of this size, holding 10,000 plants in an area measuring no more than twenty-eight yards by four yards, including the access paths between each bed. The herbaceous section, containing fewer plants, occupied a far larger area of ground. I quote these figures to show that the owner of even the smallest garden need have no fear that a plunge-bed of a size sufficient for his requirements might take up too much of his valuable space.

Although most alpine plants in the rock garden need very little watering, those in pots should be given a good soaking once a day in dry weather from late spring until early autumn. In a large commercial nursery this presents a major problem, and the manager of one such establishment where some half a million alpines are grown told me that he employed two men all day and every day doing nothing but watering his plunge-beds. With the amateur's bed holding perhaps only a couple of hundred pots, this only occupies a few minutes of the morning or evening, and he has the further advantage of being able to fix up some form of temporary shading over his small bed in hot weather. No great harm will then be done if occasionally he forgets, or is too busy, to water his plants.

Weeds are apt to be rather a nuisance in the plunge-bed and must be pulled up by hand, for of course it is impossible to use any form of weed killer when the pots are in position, and even if it is sprinkled on a vacant part of the bed some of it is sure to find its way to the roots of the eventual occupants. Slugs should be carefully watched for and are best dealt with, as already suggested, by nocturnal forays. Worms, which are beneficial in the open ground, are an unmitigated nuisance in plunge-beds, especially during the winter months, when they seem to find their way into every pot. Where plants with a compact root system are concerned they can be kept out by placing a small square of perforated zinc over the drainage hole of the pot, but this is not advisable with tap-rooted species, as their roots may eventually grow through the zinc, from which they cannot be disentangled without damage.

Little need be said about frames, whose management is probably already familiar to most of my readers. In the intensive commercial method of raising cuttings they are sited in full sun, which gives the quickest results but involves several waterings per day in hot weather. For the amateur, it is better to shade the lights, either with a proprietary wash or by tacking a square of hessian over the top of the frame. It will then be sufficient to water the cuttings in the evenings only, except perhaps during a heat-wave when an additional dose of water in the mornings will be beneficial.

The commercial nurseryman strikes his cuttings in a frame filled with sand, but here again it is advisable for the amateur to adopt a different method. If each batch of cuttings is struck in a separate pot or pan, both their insertion (which can then be carried out on the potting bench) and their subsequent management will be greatly facilitated. As soon as the cuttings are properly rooted they are potted up and removed to the hardening-off frame, which may with advantage be treated as a covered plunge-bed by half filling it with sand or ashes into which the pots are inserted. After a week or so in the closed frame they are given increasing periods of ventilation and finally moved into the open plunge-bed, where they remain until ready for planting out.

The great majority of alpine cuttings are struck in neat sand, which, of course, should be the sharpest obtainable, but for peat-loving plants the addition of a small quantity of Sorbex or some other form of clean, finely granulated peat is desirable. Since the war, increasing use has been made of a substance known as vermiculite for striking cuttings and raising seeds. This is a form of mica, and so retentive of moisture that very little watering is required. Some growers use vermiculite alone for cuttings, but as it is very loose in texture I have found it preferable to mix it with sand. Often it undoubtedly speeds up results and produces a much bushier root system than neat sand, but I have sometimes thought that cuttings rooted in this medium do not prosper so well after they have been potted up. This may, however, have been due to some other factor, and until more experience of this substance has been obtained it will not be possible to say for certain whether it is or is not beneficial. The more difficult plants can often be induced to root by the use of one of the hormone compounds such as Hortomone A or Seradix B, but this is not necessary with the easier species if they are taken at the right time of year—a point of considerable importance, which should be carefully studied.

Alpine seeds are best sown in pans, which are then covered either with glass and brown paper or, better, sheets of asbestos, which absorb the moisture and make wiping and turning unnecessary. For both seed sowing and potting it pays hands down to use the John Innes composts, which can now be purchased from most horticultural suppliers. Some amateurs, however, including myself, prefer to make up their own compost, which ensures that it is absolutely fresh and true to the John Innes formula, besides saving money if more than a very small quantity is required. It is very little trouble to make, but entails the use of a sterilizer of some kind. I have a small electric model costing only a few pounds, which is clean and easy to use and does its job most efficiently. It is plugged into a power-point in the potting shed, and when the proper emperature is reached the soil dries out and contracts, thereby breaking he circuit and switching off the apparatus.

The only difficulty to start with lies in judging the correct amount of moisture required, which varies with different kinds of soils. If the soil is too dry, the current will not pass through it; if too wet, the maximum load is soon exceeded, resulting in a blown fuse. The requisite experience is soon acquired, however, and since my first few days, when to begin with the soil remained obstinately cold and then fuses started popping like machine-guns, I have had no further trouble of any kind. There are several models on the market, and the instructions supplied by the makers should be carefully followed. Those with no previous experience of compost mixing would also be well advised to study a small book called *Seed and Potting Composts*, by W. J. C. Lawrence and J. Newell, which explains the process in detail and gives the formulae for the various John Innes mixtures. The only other equipment needed is some form of measure and a pair of scales for weighing out the chemical ingredients. I must confess to borrowing the scales from the kitchen, but unless your relations with its presiding goddess are of the most harmonious description, this plan is not to be recommended.

The propagation of alpines soon becomes a most absorbing pastime, and if his efforts during the first few seasons are attended with success, the tyro will in all probability want to extend his operations and to try his hand at the more difficult subjects. The plunge-bed-cum-frame unit can, of course, be extended indefinitely, but he may find it difficult to acquire all the information he wants from the ordinary reference books, as I did myself. Happily this has now been remedied by Mr L. D. Hills, who in 1950 produced a complete manual on the subject—the only thing of its kind, so far as I know. It is called *The Propagation of Alpines*, and contains detailed instructions for propagating virtually every alpine plant in cultivation, including a number of devices hitherto little known outside the trade. It is one of the few books which really merit that overworked epithet, 'a mine of information', and my only quarrel with the author is that he did not write it many years ago when I first began raising alpine plants.

CHAPTER SEVENTEEN

THE SINK THEME AND VARIATIONS

BROADLY SPEAKING, GARDENERS appear to be divided into two opposing camps: on the one hand, those who (prompted, one suspects, by the competitive spirit) spend their lives trying to grow bigger and better flowers; who admire dahlias as large as cartwheels and delphiniums as tall as factory chimneys: on the other, those to whom the charm of the miniature makes an irresistible appeal. I suppose there are some rational beings who manage to preserve an equilibrium between these two extremes, but most gardeners of my acquaintance show a definite bias towards one or the other.

It is fairly safe to assume that all who read these words belong to the second category, for with few exceptions the plants grown in rock gardens are small, both in stature and size of flower. Some, whose gardening activities are restricted to a backyard in the middle of a town, have smallness thrust upon them: others, with more space at their disposal, prefer small plants for their own sake. These, presumably, are actuated by that mysterious attraction which sends women into raptures over babies, puppies and kittens, and compels grown men to spend their leisure hours in constructing miniature ships, locomotives and models of the Houses Parliament. It is this fascination of the miniature, no doubt, which explains the popularity of sink and trough gardens, in which the plants are, or should be, small even by ordinary alpine standards, and minute in comparison with the general run of herbaceous perennials.

The craze for sink gardening reached its height between the wars, and to judge from the number of disused sinks to be seen in builders' yards— objects which before 1939 had assumed almost the price and rarity of collectors' pieces—it now seems to be on the wane. As so many of us today have to be content with smaller gardens than formerly, this is rather surprising, but I believe the explanation lies in a certain monotony of treatment due to lack of appreciation of the possibilities of this form of alpine gardening. Out of every hundred sink gardens one used to see, not more than one or two showed any trace of originality. By far the greater majority usually consisted of a jumbled heap of stones partially clothed with sedums: miniature editions, in fact, of Farrer's 'Almond Puddings'. Some, no doubt, had once contained their quota of choicer plants; but if so, they, like their owners, had given up the unequal struggle out of sheer boredom, probably coupled with neglect. It takes more than this to kill a sedum.

I have been a miniature garden addict ever since I first began to grow alpines, and have made quite a number of these toys, of which I still possess a few in my present garden. In making them I have always tried to keep some definite plan in view, for I can see no reason why even the smallest sink should not bear the stamp of individuality any less than a garden extending to several acres. For this reason I shall not attempt to lay down any hard-and-fast rules for such miniature layouts, but merely to indicate some of the possibilities in the hope of encouraging others to experiment on original lines.

Of receptacles for these little gardens, that most commonly met with is the old-fashioned stone sink in which the now vanished race of kitchen-maids were accustomed to do the washing-up. In many respects these are admirably suited for growing alpines, their one disadvantage being that they are rather on the shallow side. For although their other dimensions vary considerably, the depth appears to remain constant at about four inches, which is little enough when it is remembered that the lowest inch will be occupied by drainage rubble. Fortunately, however, the majority of alpines, which in their native haunts send long roots far down into the soil in quest of water, seem to flourish quite happily by spreading their root systems in a horizontal direction, so long as they can find sufficient moisture at a higher level. The lack of depth, therefore, is not such a handicap as might be supposed, and for miniature gardens of the smaller type the sink forms a very satisfactory container. Their average size is about three feet by one and a half feet, but I have one veritable monster which was actually serving its original purpose when I first came to my present house. It measures four and a half feet by two feet, and when my wife decreed its banishment in favour of a more up-to-date variety, it took several men to shift it. With the aid of rollers and levers, however, my son and I moved it all round the house to its present position on a stone bench beneath the south window of my study. It houses quite a large collection of plants of different kinds, so that throughout the spring and summer there is always something in flower to delight my eyes.

Old horse, cattle or pig troughs make excellent homes for miniature gardens on a rather larger scale, but are harder to come by than sinks and, of course, much more difficult to move about on account of their great weight. But any form of stone or pottery container may be used with success provided that it is unglazed and reasonably porous, and the choice is often limited by what is available. I have made one or two very satisfactory little gardens by using a formal layout in round earthenware vessels of the size and shape of the old-fashioned 'copper'.

Failing a ready-made receptacle, it is quite a simple job to make one, and this has the advantage that it may be of any size and shape to suit one's particular requirements. The usual method is to cast the whole thing in concrete, using a wooden mould, but unless special ingredients are employed the result is not very satisfying from the aesthetic point of view. Dr R. C., Clay, who has, or had, no less than ninety troughs and sinks of various kinds in his garden, used a mixture of crushed gravel, blue limestone chips, fine crock grit and ashes, and doubtless there are many other materials which would produce a more pleasing finish than the normal builder's concrete.

The second method, which I myself prefer, is to make a concrete base, afterwards building up the walls with small flat stones cemented together. This certainly looks better than the pre-cast trough, and the appearance can be still further enhanced by leaving a gap here and there between the stones in which small plants of trailing or creeping habit can be planted to break up the hard contours. Whichever method of construction is employed, it is a good plan to make a hole (in addition to the usual drainage hole at the bottom) some two-thirds of the way up one of the side walls, in order to drain away any surplus moisture from the crowns of the plants in winter.

Troughs, sinks and similar vessels are usually raised above ground level on stone or brick piers; an obvious advantage for those with elderly or rheumatic backs, besides helping to discourage attacks by pests of the crawling type. It is wise not to attempt to lift them straight into position, as even quite a small empty sink weighs a surprising amount, owing to the thickness of its walls. Having once succeeded in rupturing myself in this way, I now raise my sinks by placing a brick under each end, and then adding further bricks, one at a time, until the required height is reached, when the sink is manoeuvred on to its permanent support.

Miniature gardens of a rather larger and more ambitious kind may be made actually on the ground, by enclosing a small area with brick or stone walls. I have made two such gardens, the smaller of which was built up of miniature bricks of the kind used in the construction of ornamental fireplaces. This little garden, which I shall describe presently, had a strictly formal layout, or I should have preferred stones to bricks. The other, and much larger garden, was the one I have already referred to in Chapter Three, and was laid out on the lines of the large table exhibits seen at the R.H.S. shows. This type of garden offers distinct possibilities to the backyard gardener, who may be able to incorporate one or more existing walls in the fabric of the structure. The extra walls necessary to complete the rectangle need only be some two and a half or three feet high, and could be built 'dry', leaving gaps for such things as aubrietia and helianthemums in the wall face.

Details of construction, drainage, soil mixtures and so on are, of course, the same in the smallest sink as in the large rock garden in open ground, so there is no need to deal with them again. In the present chapter I am concerned only with the aesthetic angle, and it may be as well to start by drawing attention to the mistakes which so often spoil the best-intentioned efforts. The commonest of these—as in the full-sized rock garden—is the use of far too many rocks, often of an ugly or other-wise unsuitable kind and just dumped down on the surface without any apparent method or forethought. There need, of course, be no stones at all other than chippings, which should always be used as a surface dress-ing, but one or two miniature rocks are certainly useful in sinks, where they enable the gardener to build up a greater depth of soil than would be possible without them. As the cost here is negligible, only really good stones of pleasing shape and texture should be used, and the objections to limestone mentioned in an earlier chapter do not apply when the whole of the little garden is obviously artificial. Personally, I use tufa for this purpose, and find it very effective. The same attention should be paid to the correct placing and stratification of these miniature rocks as in the rock garden proper, or the result will be a miscellaneous jumble which is anything but pleasing to the eye.

Another common fault is the choice of plants which are quite unsuited to the purpose, either in the matter of height, spread or habit of growth. The smaller the garden, the more necessary it becomes for the gardener to have a good working knowledge of the plants he intends to grow; for while there are plenty of species which look ideal when received from the nurseryman, many of these will grow too large for their surroundings in the course of a season or two, and will have to be removed to more spacious quarters. This may sound obvious, but the rule that miniature gardens should contain only miniature plants is one that is all too often ignored in practice.

As far as possible I like to limit my choice to plants which do not exceed two inches in height (when in flower) for sinks, and three or four inches in the larger type of miniature garden. Their ultimate spread must also be taken into consideration, and all rampant species—except, perhaps, the dwarfest of carpeters—should be rigorously excluded. The ideal plants are those which form tight clumps, such as many of the drabas, androsaces and Kabschia saxifrages, and the following species may also be safely admitted: *Armeria caespitosa, Campanula arvatica*, the smaller dianthus species mentioned in Chapter Twelve, *Globularia bellidifolia* and *G. nana, Morisia hypogaea, Petrocallis pyrenaica, Rhodohypoxis Baurei*, and a minute viola, *V. Yakusimanii*. These may be interspersed with a few of the smaller varieties of carpeting plants such as *Hypsela longiflora, Mentha Requienii* (these last two preferring part shade), the paronychias and the raoulias, of which *R. lutescens* is the smallest and neatest, though lacking the silver foliage of *R. australis*, which I have described in Chapter Eight.

To vary the outlines, a few dwarf shrubs and trees may be included, care being taken to choose only the very smallest. Of the former, there are several genistas, micromerias and veronicas which will not be out of scale, and a delightful yellow jasmine, *Jasminum Parkeri*, should be included in all but the most miniature of gardens. Although it may ascend to some nine or twelve inches in the open garden, it does not seem to attain even half this height in the shallow soil of the sink. For a tree, nothing could be better than the smallest forms of *Chamaecyparis obtusa* already described, though *Juniperus communis compressa* will remain dwarf enough for many years, after which it can be transplanted to the open garden and replaced by a younger specimen.

Having chosen the appropriate plants, care must be taken to plant them in the appropriate places, just as when dealing with a larger garden. In the sink, it matters even less from the cultural point of view where we put them, since our dizziest summit probably rears itself no more than three or four inches above the surrounding plains, but a careful choice of sites makes all the difference to the appearance of the finished garden.

As the alpine gardener gains experience, he will probably find a special attraction in certain genera, and with the smaller species I can recommend the plan of devoting a separate sink to each genus. In this way the rarer plants can be given greater care and attention than is possible in the open garden, and they are less liable to casualties through the machination of slugs and other pests Furthermore, it enables each family of plants to be given the most suitable conditions in the way of soil, aspect and water, which is always a problem where plants of widely differing requirements are grown all together in the same sink.

The Kabschia saxifrages are ideal plants for growing in this way, and I have a sink devoted exclusively to them just outside the east window of my study. In early spring they make a lovely spectacle, which I can view in comfort without rising from my chair. On the other side of the window I have another sink full of different species of soldanellas, which, like the saxifrages, appreciate an aspect shaded from the torrid heat of the summer sun. Further afield—since they flower at a time of year when outdoor excursions are more pleasant—I have a fourth sink filled entirely with the smaller dianthus species, which like all the sun they can get. But the greatest success I have achieved in this line was a sink planted with the smaller European gentians. This was somewhat in the nature of an experiment, as I felt by no means confident that they would make themselves at home under these conditions, but they prospered surprisingly well, and indeed the lovely *G. pyrenaica* has refused to produce its purple flowers for me anywhere else. Alas! the sink was capsized by a clumsy furniture remover while I was moving house. By the time I became aware of the disaster all its inhabitants had perished, and I have never been able to replace more than a few of them.

In addition to miniature gardens of the ordinary type, there is also considerable scope for the gardener with an original turn of mind in the formal layout. I am aware that some might object to this on the grounds that it looks unnatural, but as a sink is itself severely formal in outline, I can see no reason why its contents should not follow suit. I feel sure that no one who has seen those wonderfully artistic exhibits of Miss Anne Ashbery would maintain this objection for long.

I have made one or two miniature rose and iris gardens on these lines, but my most ambitious project was the smaller of the two brick-sided enclosures already mentioned. In the centre of this was a formal pool of rather complicated shape precast in concrete and bordered by paths made of cement paving stones cast in matchbox moulds. Running the full length of these I planted miniature 'herbaceous borders' with a maximum height of some three inches, and at each corner stood a specimen of *J. communis compressa*. Unfortunately this, like various gardens I have made, both full-sized and miniature, had to be left behind when we moved house, and has no doubt long since disintegrated.

One of the most attractive gardens in miniature I have seen, though on a slightly larger scale, was made by a relative of mine on a narrow strip of turf at the edge of a lawn. It is composed entirely of evergreens—dwarf conifers and clipped hedges a foot or so high enclosing little lawns (which are mown with nail scissors). This once gave me the idea of constructing a miniature replica of my entire garden, until I realised that the model, being situated within the garden, would have to contain a yet smaller edition of itself, and so on *ad infinitum* like the fleas in the old rhyme: a nightmare thought!

For the average gardener, however, the sink will probably remain the most popular form of miniature garden, and its ease of management, in such matters as watering and winter protection, give it most of the advantages of the alpine house without the expense of the latter. If the soil is surfaced with stone chippings, as it should be, watering through a rosed can is quite satisfactory except with plants which dislike getting their heads wet (e.g. *Draba mollissima.*) In troughs containing plants of this kind, therefore, I sink a few short lengths of small-bore piping, through which water is poured direct on to the drainage until the whole of the soil is thoroughly soaked. An alternative method, if the garden contains a small cement pond, is to water through a hole in the bottom of this, afterwards closing it with a plug. But in whatever manner the water is applied, a cork should be inserted beforehand and subsequently removed in order to allow the surplus moisture to drain away. I have also tried cementing a tap into the bottom of the sink, which is very convenient until it is required to move the little garden, when it becomes a decided drawback.

With regard to protection from the winter rains, the ideal method would be to have a small frame made to fit over each sink with a light which could be opened on dry sunny days. As this would be rather an expensive proposition, however, I use ordinary cloches instead. Unfortunately the standard tent type is just too narrow for the average sink and the barn type just too wide, but this difficulty is easily overcome by constructing a rough wooden frame on which the base of a barn cloche can rest.

The cloches should be lashed down very securely, as the glass end pieces supplied cannot be used in a sink to prevent them from being lifted by the wind. A few years ago, on the night after I had secured my cloches in place for the winter, a strong south-westerly gale sprang up, but feeling confident of the security of my lashings, I retired to bed without a qualm. I was awakened at midnight by a series of frightful crashes beneath my bedroom window, and the morning light revealed a devastating scene of carnage, in which bits of cord and broken glass were mingled in inextricable confusion with the slashed and sodden tufts of my cherished alpines. The wind had evidently lifted the cloches just enough to permit them to 'work', and the resultant friction had gradually chafed through my stout cords. Since then I have used old telephone wire to secure the glass on my sinks, and I can now sleep through the fiercest gale undisturbed by thoughts of further expensive catastrophes.

CHAPTER EIGHTEEN

WINDOWSILL GARDENING

As a matter of general principle, I must confess myself opposed to the pot cultivation of alpine plants. The spectacle of these wildlings imprisoned in pots or pans and trotted round from show to show chiefly for the purpose of displaying their owners' skill and to compete for prizes, has much the same effect upon me as an exhibition of caged wild birds, though of course in a lesser degree. Maybe this is a foolish and sentimental notion, but I know there are a great many alpine enthusiasts who share my views on the matter.

Nevertheless, there are certain alpines flowering in the early spring which, for one reason or another, do not give of their best in the rock garden, and these I can and do enjoy on the windowsill of my study without a twinge of conscience. Some of these are wild species but many are garden forms in which the hand of the hybridist has played its part, which, for reasons which it is hard to explain but which every alpine fancier will recognize, still further absolves me from offence. For this purpose, however, I confine myself to those plants which bloom at the time of year when there is little temptation to linger out-of-doors, and a bright display in my window is therefore all the more welcome.

For those who go in extensively for the pot cultivation of alpines a specially fitted greenhouse is necessary, with a double row of ventilators running the full length on each side, roller blinds for shading purposes, and various other refinements. These fittings, however, are chiefly required during the summer months, when the ordinary cold house becomes much too hot for plants from the high hills. For those who merely want to keep a few alpines to brighten their windowsills in early spring, any unheated greenhouse, or even a small frame or a few cloches, will suffice, since the chief purpose of the glass is to protect the plants from winter rain.

In order to avoid possible disappointment, I must make it clear at the outset that although, given the right conditions, quite a number of alpine plants can safely be brought indoors, it is too much to expect them to thrive in the stuffy atmosphere of a modern centrally-heated flat, though a few of them may even put up with this for a short time. Accustomed as they are in their native haunts to spend the winter beneath a thick blanket of snow and the summer exposed to all the fresh air of the mountains, they will not submit to being treated as hothouse plants, however accommodating they may be in other ways.

In this respect—though admittedly in few others—the old-fashioned ex-rectory which is my home has its advantages, for the conditions indoors during the winter are scarcely different from those of a cold greenhouse. Indeed, my study, which possesses several large windows and no form of heating except an ancient brick fireplace which smokes too badly to be used, bears a strong resemblance to a giant refrigerator. The modern flat-dweller, I am afraid, would consider it quite unfit for human habitation; but when, during an exceptionally cold spell, the ink congeals on my pen and the thoughts in my brain, I console myself with the reflection that, at all events, the alpines on my windowsill are enjoying themselves.

Different species, however, vary in their reactions to indoor life, so unless your living room becomes abnormally sultry, it is worth trying a few of them to see how they take to it. If necessary, they could be brought indoors each morning and returned to the greenhouse or frame in the evening, when the heat of the room is usually increased and their colouring is lost, in any case, under the artificial light. If despite these precautions, some of the plants showed signs of flagging after a few days, a longer spell outside would restore them to health. But, having spent most of my life in old country houses and being without any first-hand experience of rooms fitted with draught-proof windows and modern heating appliances, I am in no position to offer detailed advice on this point.

With regard to the most suitable plants for the window display, there is, to my mind, nothing to beat the Kabschia saxifrages, which I have already described in some detail in Chapter Nine. They can, of course, be quite easily grown in the open garden, but as they flower in February and March their delicate blooms are as often as not reduced to a tattered, soil-splashed pulp by the onslaught of the English climate. I therefore hold it no sacrilege to grow them under conditions in which they can develop their full beauty, and a row of them on my windowsill in various shades of red, pink, yellow and white never fails to elicit the admiration of my visitors.

Among the vast host of primula there are a number of delightful early-flowering species and hybrids well suited to our purpose. I am conscious of having said some rather unkind things about this great genus, so I will now do my best to make amends. The one which pleases me most is *P. Clarkei*, a miniature primrose with crinkly green leaves and almost stemless flowers of the most brilliant shade of carmine-rose. Although

known to Farrer, this primula has only recently come into general cultivation, but has become very popular with alpine enthusiasts since the
war. Like most of the Asiatic species it prefers a cool spot; so, while it
is quite happy in the arctic conditions of my study, I am afraid a heated
room might prove too much for it.

Probably the best primulas for the average windowsill are those from
the mountains of Europe, such as *P. marginata*, an easy and attractive
plant with flowers of lavender-blue. It has several garden forms, of which
Linda Pope is generally considered the best. Another good group are the
hybrids known collectively as *P. ×pubescens*. These are descended on one
side from *P. auricula*, which was also responsible for the florist's 'auri-
culas', to which *P. × pubescens* bears a strong family resemblance. There
are several named varieties on the market, of which the old favourite
Mrs J. H. Wilson, with flowers of rich purple, is still one of the best. The
General is a good bright red, as befits his rank, and there is a pleasing
white form, *P. × p. alba*. Among the many wild species of primula the
beautiful *P. Allionii* has achieved the greatest popularity as a pot plant
and is always to the fore at the alpine shows, but as this is rather more
difficult to grow than the others I have named, perhaps we had better
leave it and others of its kindred to the experts with their alpine houses.
The primulas flower rather later than the Kabschia saxifrages, but when
grown under glass those I have named should bloom during April, which
is the closing month for my windowsill garden.

If I was asked to name a characteristic plant of the European alps my
thoughts would instinctively turn to the soldanella—or rather, soldanellas, for there are half a dozen species in this small but select genus. Indeed, they are such typical children of the hills that I should never im-
prison them in pans but for the difficulty of persuading them to bloom
out of doors, and for the same reason I did not include them in my
chapter on Alpines of Charm and Distinction, in which they would otherwise have occupied a prominent place. Farrer suggested that their bad
reputation in this important respect might be due to slugs or mice eating
their buds rather than to any shortcomings of the plants themselves,
which in their native Alps flower with considerable freedom. Whether
this is actually true I rather doubt, as if the truth be told they are little,
if anything, more forthcoming in the sinks and pans in which I have
grown them for some years past. However, I prefer not to take any
chances, and on the comparatively rare occasions when they do con-
descend to produce their flowers I prefer that I and my friends, rather
than the local fauna, should have the benefit of them.

Campanula muralis

Dianthus glacialis

The six species, between which there are also several hybrids, are *SS. alpina, hungarica, minima, montana, pindicola* and *pusilla*, of which the first is the most commonly encountered in catalogues and at the flower shows. I have tried them all except the second, and although they are perfectly easy to grow, *S. montana* is the only one which flowers for me with any degree of freedom and regularity. *SS. alpina* and *pusilla* have produced a few flowers in some seasons but not in others; *SS. minima* and *pindicola*, never up to the time of writing. They are all rather similar in appearance, and bear—or ought to bear—the most charming fringed bells of lavender or lilac above mats of round, rich green leaves. The chief difference between them is one of size, *S. montana* being the largest and *S. minima* the smallest.

Of a very different class, but with attractions of their own, are those plants which a well-known alpine nurseryman terms 'buns', from the compact, rounded shape of their clumps when out of flower. The genus draba furnishes a number of typical examples, of which *D. mollissima* has become a great favourite with alpine exhibitors in recent years. Although grown chiefly for the sake of its neat grey-green hummocks, it covers itself in March or April with numerous bright yellow flowers on slender stalks, the general effect being that of a pincushion studded with yellow-headed pins. It so hates winter damp that it is next to impossible to keep through the winter in the open garden, which fully justifies its cultivation in a pot or pan.

This draba needs very careful watering, with little or no water at all throughout the winter, and in autumn it always frightens me by turning completely brown. A close examination, however, reveals a minute point of green in the centre of the majority of its rosettes, and these will burgeon again in the following spring. Those which do not show any trace of green will die and form an ugly brown patch on the cushion, but if these dead parts are carefully cut out and the whole plant slightly raised by pushing small pieces of stone underneath it, the living foliage will close the gap and by midsummer the wound will be scarcely noticeable. *D. polytricha* is a somewhat similar plant but with larger rosettes, and *D. bryoides imbricata* is a good representative of the green-leaved species. Closely allied to the drabas, and now sometimes listed under their generic name, is *Petrocallis pyrenaica*, a most attractive dwarf with scented lilac flowers, borne a month or so later than those of the true drabas.

The androsaces include some delightful plants for growing in pots, but unfortunately the most attractive of these, with bun-shaped cushions, are rather too pernickety for most of us, while others flower too late for our present purpose. *AA. carnea* and *villosa*, together with their varieties, are, however, easy and pleasant little plants which are worth their place in the spring windowsill garden.

From the drabas and androsaces it is a far cry to that strange and very different plant, *Parochetus communis*, from the Himalayas, which I have already briefly described among the True Blues of the alpine world. As it is not entirely hardy, you can only be certain of enjoying its brilliant flowers by growing it under glass. It produces these in unending succession from October to February, and is therefore particularly welcome in the dark days of winter when all the other alpines are asleep. As it likes a warm situation it is a very suitable subject for bringing into the house, but it should be kept amply supplied with water, for which, with its abundance of lush green foliage to support, it has an insatiable thirst. It should be kept as close to the light as possible, or it will become drawn up and spindly. Under suitable conditions it spreads very rapidly, and after two or three seasons will require the largest pan available. If smaller specimens are required, one has only to pull off a few rooted pieces and put them into pots, when they will form sizeable plants in a very short time.

There are plenty of other alpine plants which can be successfully grown in pots, but beyond one or two special treasures of uncertain temper, I exclude from my windowsill all those which flower after the end of April, when I can enjoy them better in the open garden. I must, however, make some mention of bulbs, which have not so far appeared in this book because the dividing line between rock garden and other bulbs is too nebulous for definition. Most people grow at least a few spring bulbs in fibre, but these are usually the taller hybrids of narcissus, hyacinth and tulip, which to my eyes always look rather top-heavy in bowls. I much prefer the small species, of which there is a wide choice among the chionodoxas, crocuses (the true species, not the bloated garden forms), erythroniums, fritillarias, irises and narcissi. Some of the last-named are particularly attractive and seem to thrive better in pans than in the open. They should not be grown in fibre or forced in any way, but potted up in ordinary compost and kept in a cold house or frame until they are ready to be brought indoors.

The great majority of alpines can be grown successfully in the John Innes potting compost, though the cushion-forming plants, such as the Kabschia saxifrages, drabas and androsaces, appreciate an extra ration of grit, for which there is nothing better than finely crushed crocks. These are easily mass-produced by smashing up a heap of old broken flower-pots with a coal hammer and passing the resulting debris through a sieve.

Those who wish to grow a large number of alpines in this way should consult Mr Stuart Boothman's admirable little book, *The Alpine House*, which sets out the individual requirements of each plant in detail.

Watering is the most difficult problem which those who grow alpines in pots have to face, and in its correct solution lies more than half the secret of success. Unfortunately this knowledge cannot be learned from books, but must be acquired by practical experience aided by observation and common-sense. Broadly speaking, plants with luxuriant green foliage need more water than those forming tight cushions, but their requirements vary not only from species to species but also according to such changeable factors as weather and temperature. Nearly all alpines want plenty of water in the growing season, the supply being gradually reduced as autumn approaches until, during the winter months, they are watered only very occasionally until they start into growth once more. A small watering-can holding about two pints is necessary for dealing with small pots, and it should have a long spout through which the water is poured (without the rose) directly on to the stone chippings with which the pans should be surfaced. When watering the woolly-leaved species such as *Draba mollissima*, care should be taken not to splash the foliage.

The plants are brought indoors from the cold house or frame when the buds begin to expand, and unless they show signs of wilting they can be kept on the windowsill until the flowers fade. The best place for them throughout the summer months is the plunge-bed, along with the young potted stuff whose waterings they then share. If no nursery bed is available it is an easy matter to dig a small trench and to fill this with sand or ashes in which the pans are plunged. Here they remain until the fogs and rain of autumn dictate their removal to a position under glass once more.

The actual method of staging the windowsill display is, of course, a matter of individual taste. I use separate pots or pans of the appropriate size for each plant, but on a broad sill a good effect could be obtained by using larger pans holding several plants apiece, or even a long earthenware trough arranged like a miniature garden. As the receptacles make rather a mess of paintwork, it is advisable to stand them in saucers, which also serve to catch the surplus water seeping through the drainage holes. Last winter my wife found, in a fancy goods shop, a long rectangular basket with a metal lining, which makes an admirable container for half a dozen 3-inch pots and has the advantage of enabling the plants to be watered *in situ*. There are, however, plenty of possibilities in windowsill arrangement which I have not yet explored, and the ingenious reader

will no doubt find his own solution according to the size and shape of
his windowsills and the vessels at his disposal.

I conclude this chapter, and with it my book, as the last day of 1953
is drawing to a close. In a few minutes from now the bells in the village
church which adjoins my garden will be announcing the arrival of
January, and I shall be able to say 'Next month my Kabschia saxifrages
will be in flower'. From then onwards there will be a continuous and
ever-increasing display of bloom, first on my windowsill and later in the
rock garden, for many months to come: a thought which brings no small
comfort on a dark December night.

INDEX